goodFOOD

Best Ever
Slow Cooker Recipes

First published in Great Britain in 2026 by Hamlyn, an imprint of Octopus Publishing Group Ltd
Carmelite House
50 Victoria Embankment
London EC4Y 0DZ
www.octopusbooks.co.uk

An Hachette UK Company
www.hachette.co.uk

The authorized representative in the EEA is Hachette Ireland, 8 Castlecourt Centre, Dublin 15, D15 XTP3, Ireland (email: info@hbgi.ie)

The recipes in this book have previously appeared on the *Good Food* website.

Distributed in the US by Hachette Book Group, 1290 Avenue of the Americas, 4th and 5th Floors, New York, NY 10104

Distributed in Canada by Canadian Manda Group, 664 Annette St., Toronto, Ontario, Canada M6S 2C8

ISBN: 978-0-600-64033-2
eISBN: 978-0-600-64043-1

A CIP catalogue record for this book is available from the British Library.

Printed and bound in China.

10 9 8 7 6 5 4 3 2 1

Publisher: Kate Fox
Creative Director: Jonathan Christie
Senior Editor: Leanne Bryan
Assistant Editor: Alice Gawthrop
Project Editor: Sarah Reece
Designer: Nicky Collings
Assistant Production Manager: Lisa Pinnell

At *Good Food* magazine:
Commercial Director: Simon Carrington
Food Editor & Test Kitchen Manager: Alice Shields
Head of Brand Trust: Lulu Grimes
Art Director: Rachel Bayly
Head of Food: Cassie Best

FSC www.fsc.org MIX Paper | Supporting responsible forestry FSC® C008047

goodFOOD

Best Ever Slow Cooker Recipes

100 SIMPLE, AFFORDABLE, PREP-AHEAD RECIPES

hamlyn

Cooks' notes

All the recipes have been triple tested in the Good Food development kitchen and nutritionally analysed by a qualified nutritionist.

Recipes contain nutritional analyses for 'sugar', which means the total sugar content including all natural sugars in the ingredients unless otherwise stated.

Spoon measurements are level unless otherwise specified.

1 teaspoon (tsp) = 5ml

1 tablespoon (tbsp) = 15ml

Both imperial and metric measurements have been given in all recipes. Conversions are approximate and have been rounded up or down. Use one set of measurements only and not a mixture of both.

Wash fresh produce before preparation.

Pepper should be freshly ground black pepper unless otherwise stated.

ICON KEY

- ✱ *Freezable*
- V *Vegetarian*
- Ve *Vegan*

Milk should be semi-skimmed, unless otherwise specified.

Eggs should be medium unless otherwise stated. The UK's Food Standards Agency (FSA) advises that raw or lightly cooked hen eggs or foods containing them may be consumed if they have a British Lion mark or are produced under the Laid in Britain egg assurance scheme. This advice does not apply to individuals who are severely immunocompromised and require medically supervised diets prescribed by health professionals. The US Department of Agriculture (USDA) advises everyone against eating raw or undercooked eggs, but in-shell eggs that have been pasteurized may be used safely without cooking.

This book includes dishes made with **nuts** and nut derivatives. It is advisable for customers with known allergic reactions to nuts and nut derivatives and those who may be potentially vulnerable to these allergies, such as babies and children with a family history of allergies, to avoid dishes made with nuts and nut oils. It is also prudent to check the labels of pre-prepared ingredients for the possible inclusion of nut derivatives.

Vegetarians should look for the 'V' symbol on a **cheese** to ensure it is made with a vegetarian rennet.

CONTENTS

Introduction

For many of us, the idea of a home-cooked meal on a busy weeknight can feel like an unachievable luxury. But a slow cooker can offer the perfect hands-off solution – just a few minutes of prep in the morning and you can come home to the comforting smell of a warm and enticing dinner that will be on the table in a flash.

Slow cookers are much loved for their practicality and convenience, but there is no compromise on the quality of the finished dish. In fact, the low-and-slow cook is the very best way to achieve great results with stews, curries, casseroles and braises, resulting in melt-in-the-mouth tender meat and vegetables in rich sauces with great depth of flavour.

In this book, we've compiled our best ever slow cooker recipes to suit every occasion – from weeknight classics and fakeaway favourites, to crowd-pleasing centrepieces and effortless comfort food. And don't forget dessert! There are plenty of sweet treats to choose from too, such as moist sticky toffee pudding, saucy chocolate fondant cake and easy fudge – all made even simpler thanks to the slow cooker.

Every single recipe includes clear, detailed instructions for preparing and cooking, so you'll know what to do every step of the way.

How slow cookers work

Electric slow cookers first rose to popularity in the 1970s but have enjoyed a resurgence in recent years as a low-effort solution for time-strapped cooks. The concept of slow cooking, however, is nothing new. For millennia, humans have been cooking meat and vegetables for long periods of time over indirect heat sources such as barbecue pits until they are moist and tender.

Slow cookers work by simmering food at a low temperature over several hours, which makes them ideal for cooking your dinner while you are out for the day. They're incredibly simple to use and often require simply plugging in and switching on. The ceramic pot in which the food is cooked creates an enclosed environment that helps to trap the steam and keep food moist.

Most models offer two temperature settings: low and high. The difference between these settings is the time it takes the slow cooker to come up to a simmer rather than a different level of heat. Most dishes work best on the low setting, ideal for bringing out the flavours and tenderizing any meat. The high setting works best for ingredients like pasta and rice, which may become soggy if cooked for an extended period of time.

Some slow cookers have a sear function that allows you to brown the ingredients to add all-important flavour before the slow cook. If yours has this function, you can sear your ingredients in your slow cooker rather than in a frying pan on the hob if this is part of the recipe's method.

How to use your slow cooker

LARGE OR SMALL?

Slow cookers vary in size, which is why most recipes contain a cooking time range. The majority of recipes will work in any size of slow cooker, but if yours is particularly small, you may need to scale down any dishes that use a large quantity of liquid. If you're using a large slow cooker, check the dish after the lower amount of cooking time suggested, then continue to cook for a little longer, if necessary.

DON'T OVERFILL

Don't be tempted to fill your slow cooker to the brim. Two-thirds full is about right to ensure even cooking and avoid overspilling.

USING FROZEN INGREDIENTS

Make sure you defrost any meat or poultry before adding them to your slow cooker, as frozen meat will take longer to reach a safe internal temperature. Frozen ingredients will also cool everything else in the slow cooker, resulting in a longer cooking time.

THICKENING A SAUCE

Cooking juices don't thicken up as much in a slow cooker, as the water cannot evaporate away, so toss meat in a couple of tablespoons of flour before cooking, if needed. Alternatively, thicken with cornflour 'slurry' (a mixture of cornflour and a little water) at the end of cooking. For thicker sauces, you may have to transfer the whole dish, or just strain some of the liquid off, into a pan and bubble over a high heat to reduce before serving.

Ultimate convenience

For many people, the slow cooker has transformed their mealtimes. After a little bit of prep in the morning, and a long slow cook all day while they are at work, they have a hot and tempting dinner on the table minutes after walking through the door. And if they double up the ingredients or have leftovers, they have extra delicious home-cooked meals in the fridge or freezer just waiting to be defrosted and reheated.

If you're in a rush in the mornings, you can of course just bung all the ingredients straight in the slow cooker and switch it on. However, many of the recipes in this book suggest browning ingredients such as onions and meat in a frying pan on the hob first to add an extra layer of flavour. This isn't essential, however – this step can be missed if you are short on time. If you don't have time to fry them, grate onions rather than chop them to help them cook down into the sauce.

If you know you are heading for a busy week, you can get ahead even further by portioning raw ingredients into a 'dump box' for each recipe and freezing them. Defrost fully in the fridge before 'dumping' into your slow cooker. Be sure to use reusable freezerproof containers.

Making the most of your ingredients

- To save using an extra pan to cook your carbs, stir dried pasta, noodles or rice into stews or casseroles in the slow cooker about 20 minutes before the end of the cooking time. You may need to add in a little extra water, as they'll soak up some of the liquid. Turn up the heat to high so that they cook through before becoming mushy.

- To avoid overcooking, layer quicker-cooking ingredients such as prawns on top of the vegetables so that they're further away from the heat source.

- Add more tender vegetables towards the end of the cooking time to avoid them overcooking and losing texture.

- If the recipe calls for it, stir in cream just for the final 30 minutes of cooking, to avoid it overheating and splitting.

- Skinless chicken works best for many recipes because no matter how long you cook it, the skin simply won't crisp up in the steamy environment of the slow cooker. However, if you want the flavour the skin adds, simply grill the chicken to crisp up the skin after cooking in the slow cooker.

Budget tips

Slow cookers lend themselves to cooking cheaper cuts of meat because the low-and-slow cook breaks down the tough fibres and collagen, and the moist environment prevents them from drying out. In fact, the very best stews and casseroles use these cheaper cuts because the end result is simply better than more expensive, leaner cuts: the meat becomes so tender that it falls off the bone and the sauce is rich and unctuous.

Other economical ingredients such as root vegetables, beans and pulses also work particularly well in a slow cooker, as the gentle approach ensures they become tender, not mushy. These ingredients are great for bulking out casseroles, soups, even lasagne, so you can cut down on more expensive meat.

Slow cookers are the ultimate gadget for batch cooking, which is a cheap and convenient way to feed the family, or even just yourself. Cook batches of curries and chilli to fill the fridge and freezer for the week ahead. Defrost fully in the fridge before reheating on the hob until piping hot.

Getting started

There are many different reasons why people love their slow cookers. For some, it's the convenience of preparing their evening meal in the morning when they have more energy so that they can simply get on with their day. For others, it's the joy of coming home to a comforting meal they wouldn't otherwise have time to cook.

Some people use their slow cooker as a convenient way to batch cook, filling the freezer with ready-to-eat meals. Others appreciate the convenient hands-off approach to cooking cheaper meats and vegetables.

Everyone loves the results that the low-and-slow cooking process brings to their dishes.

Let's get started! With over a hundred reliable and delicious recipes in this book, both sweet and savoury, now is a good time to get your slow cooker out of the cupboard and put it to use in your kitchen.

Midweek Meals

Chicken Chasseur

Prep: 15 mins
Cook: 6 hrs and 35 mins–8 hrs and 35 mins

Serves 2

2 tbsp olive oil
4 bone-in, skin-on chicken thighs
2 shallots or 1 onion, finely chopped
2 garlic cloves, crushed
200g (7oz) baby chestnut mushrooms, halved
200ml (7fl oz) white wine
1 tbsp tomato purée
200g (7oz) canned chopped tomatoes
2 thyme sprigs
1 bay leaf
400ml (14fl oz) hot chicken stock
small handful of finely chopped parsley
mashed potato, pasta or roast potatoes, to serve

1 Put the oil in a frying pan over a medium–high heat. Season the chicken and fry, skin side down, for 4–5 mins until crisp. Turn and fry for 3–4 mins more until golden all over. Put on a plate and set aside.

2 Tip the shallots or onion into the pan and fry for 10 mins over a medium heat until soft. Add the garlic and mushrooms and fry for 10 mins more until the mushrooms are golden. Pour in the wine and bubble for a few minutes until reduced by half. Stir in the tomato purée, chopped tomatoes and herbs. Season well and bring to a simmer.

3 Tip the sauce into your slow cooker and top with the chicken thighs (in one layer, if possible). Pour over the chicken stock until the chicken thighs are covered, adding a little more if needed. Cover and cook on low for 6–8 hrs until the sauce has thickened and the chicken is tender. Transfer the chicken to a plate and bubble the sauce for a few minutes more with the lid off if you prefer a thicker sauce. (You can only do this if there's a reduce function on the slow cooker. If not, pour the sauce into a saucepan and simmer until reduced.)

4 Sprinkle over the parsley and serve the chicken and sauce with buttery mashed potato, pasta or small roast potatoes.

NUTRITIONAL INFO

PER SERVING KCAL **485** | FAT **26G** | SATURATES **6G** | CARBS **15G** | SUGARS **12G** | FIBRE **4G** | PROTEIN **29G** | SALT **1.4G**

Butter Chicken Curry

Prep: 25 mins, plus marinating
Cook: 6 hrs and 15 mins–7 hrs and 15 mins

Serves 4

500g (1lb 2oz) boneless, skinless chicken thighs, cut into 3 pieces
2 tbsp butter, ghee or vegetable oil
1 large onion, chopped
3 garlic cloves, crushed
1 green chilli, deseeded and finely chopped (optional)
thumb-sized piece of ginger, peeled and grated
1 tsp garam masala
2 tsp ground fenugreek
3 tbsp tomato purée
250ml (9fl oz) chicken stock
50g (1¾ oz) toasted flaked almonds

For the marinade

juice of 1 lemon
2 tsp ground cumin
2 tsp paprika
1–2 tsp hot chilli powder
200ml (7fl oz) natural yogurt

To serve

basmati rice
naan
mango chutney or lime pickle
coriander
lime wedges (optional)

1. In a medium bowl, mix all the marinade ingredients with some seasoning. Toss the chicken with the marinade, cover and chill in the fridge for 1 hr or overnight.
2. In a large, heavy saucepan, heat the butter, ghee or oil. Add the onion, garlic, green chilli, if using, ginger and some seasoning. Fry on a medium heat for 10 mins or until soft.
3. Add the spices with the tomato purée and cook for a further 2 mins until fragrant, then add the stock and marinated chicken. Tip everything into your slow cooker, then cover and cook on low for 6–7 hrs until the chicken is tender.
4. Sprinkle with the toasted almonds and serve with rice, naan, chutney or lime pickle, coriander and lime wedges for squeezing over, if you like.

NUTRITIONAL INFO

PER SERVING KCAL **371** | FAT **19G** | SATURATES **7G** | CARBS **11G** | SUGARS **10G** | FIBRE **3G** | PROTEIN **36G** | SALT **0.79G**

Tasty Turkey Meatballs

Prep: 30 mins
Cook: 5 hrs and 15 mins

Serves 4–5

1 tbsp rapeseed oil
1 onion, finely chopped
2 carrots, finely chopped
2 celery sticks, finely chopped
2 garlic cloves, thinly sliced
500ml (18fl oz) passata
2 tbsp chopped parsley, plus extra to garnish
pasta, rice or green salad, to serve

For the meatballs

400g (14oz) lean minced turkey
4 tbsp porridge oats
pinch of paprika
1 garlic clove, crushed
1 tbsp olive oil

1. Heat the oil in a nonstick frying pan, add the onion, carrots, celery and garlic and fry gently for 5–10 mins until softened. Pour in the passata, add the parsley and stir, then transfer everything to your slow cooker.
2. To make the meatballs, tip the minced turkey into a large bowl. Add the oats, paprika, garlic and plenty of black pepper and mix everything together with your hands. Divide the mixture into 20 lumps about the size of a walnut and roll each piece into a meatball. Heat the oil in a nonstick frying pan and gently cook the meatballs until they start to brown.
3. Add the meatballs to the tomato base, cover the slow cooker with the lid and cook on low for 5 hrs.
4. Sprinkle with parsley and serve over pasta or rice or with a green salad.

NUTRITIONAL INFO

PER SERVING (IF SERVING 4) KCAL **277** | FAT **6G** | SATURATES **1G** | CARBS **22G** | SUGARS **11G** | FIBRE **6G** | PROTEIN **29G** | SALT **0.39G**

✳

Tender Beef Brisket

Prep: 30 mins
Cook: 7 hrs and 30 mins – 8 hrs and 30 mins

Serves 6

1.2kg (2lb 10oz) brisket, rolled
2 tbsp vegetable oil, plus extra for drizzling
2 large onions, sliced
4 tbsp plain flour
500–550ml (18–19fl oz) golden ale
1 tbsp yeast or beef extract
1 tbsp dark brown soft sugar, plus extra to taste
1 tbsp balsamic vinegar, plus extra to taste
½ bunch of thyme
2 bay leaves
500ml (18fl oz) hot beef stock
2 tsp cornflour (optional)

For the horseradish mash
2kg (4lb 8oz) Maris Piper or other floury potatoes, chopped
4 tbsp horseradish
100g (3½oz) butter
100ml (3½fl oz) crème fraîche
handful of parsley, chopped

1 Season the brisket all over with salt and pepper. Heat the vegetable oil in a frying pan and sear the meat all over until browned. Transfer to a plate. Add another drizzle of oil, if needed, and fry the onions with a pinch of salt for about 12 mins until lightly golden. Sprinkle over the flour and stir until well mixed, then pour in the ale and scrape the bottom of the pan to pick up any browned bits. Tip everything into your slow cooker.

2 Add the yeast or beef extract, sugar and vinegar, then the brisket and herbs. Top up with stock until the brisket is submerged just over halfway. Cover and cook on low for 7–8 hrs until tender. Remove the brisket from the slow cooker and cover to keep warm. Use the reduce or simmer function on the slow cooker and simmer for 10–15 mins until the gravy has thickened to your liking. If the slow cooker doesn't have a reduce function, pour the gravy into a saucepan and simmer on the hob until thickened. Add a pinch more salt or sugar or a dash more vinegar if needed. If you like your gravy to be extra thick, mix the cornflour with a splash of cold water, then add to the pan and bubble for a few minutes.

3 Just before you remove the brisket from the slow cooker, start on the mash. Cook the potatoes in a pan of salted boiling water for 20 mins until very tender when pressed. Drain and steam-dry for a few minutes before mashing with the horseradish, butter and crème fraîche. Scatter with the parsley to serve.

4 Cut the brisket into wedges and serve with the gravy and mash.

5 Once cooled, you can freeze the brisket and gravy together in an airtight container for up to three months. Defrost thoroughly in the fridge, then reheat on low in your slow cooker or in a low oven until piping hot.

NUTRITIONAL INFO
PER SERVING KCAL **928** | FAT **47G** | SATURATES **22G** | CARBS **74G** | SUGARS **14G** | FIBRE **8G** | PROTEIN **45G** | SALT **1.3G**

Beef Bourguignon

Prep: 20 mins
Cook: 6 hrs and 30 mins–8 hrs and 30 mins

Serves 6–8

3 tbsp vegetable oil
1.5kg (3lb 5oz) stewing steak, cut into small chunks
2 large onions, chopped
2 carrots, chopped
2 celery sticks, chopped
2 bay leaves
2 thyme or rosemary sprigs
3 tbsp plain flour
750ml (1⅓ pints) red wine
1 beef stock cube
1 tsp golden caster sugar
2 tbsp tomato purée
100g (3½ oz) unsmoked bacon rashers, chopped
6 small shallots or baby onions, halved if large
300g (10½oz) closed cup mushrooms, halved or quartered
mashed potato or crusty bread, to serve

1 Heat 2 tbsp oil in a large frying pan. Season the meat and fry for 3–4 mins in batches until browned all over, scooping out each batch with a slotted spoon and transferring the browned meat to a plate.

2 Tip the onions, carrots and celery into the pan and fry for 5–10 mins until soft. Add the herbs and flour and cook for another 2 mins. Pour a splash of the wine into a bowl, then add the stock cube, sugar and tomato purée and mix to form a paste. Scrape the paste into the onion mix and pour in the remaining wine. Bring the mixture to a bubble, then transfer to your slow cooker. Stir in the browned beef, topping up with a splash of water to cover the meat if needed. Cover with the lid and cook on low for 6–8 hrs until the meat is very tender.

3 About 35 mins before serving, heat the remaining oil in a pan. Fry the bacon, shallots or baby onions and mushrooms for 5–8 mins until caramelized and the veg is starting to soften, then tip into the slow cooker. Cook the stew on high for 30 mins. If you want a thicker gravy, use the reduce function or leave the stew uncovered. Serve with mashed potato or crusty bread.

NUTRITIONAL INFO

PER SERVING (IF SERVING 8) KCAL **497** | FAT **20G** | SATURATES **7G** | CARBS **14G** | SUGARS **7G** | FIBRE **3G** | PROTEIN **47G** | SALT **1G**

Beef Bolognese

Prep: 15 mins
Cook: 7 hrs and 30 mins–9 hrs and 30 mins

Serves 12

4 tbsp olive oil
6 smoked bacon rashers, chopped
1.5kg (3lb 5oz) lean minced beef (or use half beef, half pork)
4 onions, finely chopped
3 carrots, finely chopped
4 celery sticks, finely chopped
8 garlic cloves, crushed
500g (1lb 2oz) mushrooms, sliced
4 × 400g (14oz) cans chopped tomatoes
6 tbsp tomato purée
2 tbsp dried mixed herbs
2 bay leaves
large glass of red wine (optional)
4 tbsp red wine vinegar
1 tbsp golden caster sugar

To serve
spaghetti
parmesan

1 Heat the oil in a large pan and fry the bacon and minced beef in batches until browned. Add to your slow cooker.

2 Add all the remaining ingredients and seasoning to the slow cooker. Cover and cook on low for 6–8 hrs, then uncover, turn to high and cook for another hour until thick and saucy.

3 Serve with spaghetti and shaved or grated parmesan.

4 Once cooled, the beef bolognese will keep frozen in an airtight container for up to two months. Defrost thoroughly in the fridge and reheat until piping hot.

NUTRITIONAL INFO

PER SERVING KCAL **295** | FAT **12G** | SATURATES **4G** | CARBS **13G** | SUGARS **11G** | FIBRE **4G** | PROTEIN **34G** | SALT **0.87G**

✳ V Ve

Prep: 20 mins
Cook: 5 hrs and 30 mins–6 hrs and 30 mins

Spiced Root & Lentil Casserole

Serves 4

- 2 tbsp olive oil
- 1 onion, finely chopped
- 3 carrots, peeled and cut into chunks
- 500g (1lb 2oz) parsnips, peeled and cut into chunks
- 3 garlic cloves, crushed
- 2 tbsp mild curry powder
- 1 tbsp smoked paprika
- 150g (5½ oz) dried red lentils, rinsed
- 600ml (20fl oz) hot vegetable stock
- 2 bay leaves
- lemon juice, to taste
- crusty bread, to serve (optional)

TIP

This recipe is ideal for a 3.5 litre (6 pint) slow cooker. If yours is larger, double the quantities and freeze the leftovers.

1. Heat the oil in a frying pan and cook the onion for 10 mins until soft and translucent. Add the carrots and parsnips and fry for 8–10 mins until the veg is just golden. Stir in the garlic and spices and fry for 4–5 mins until fragrant, stirring. Add a splash of water if needed. Tip into your slow cooker. Stir through the lentils, stock, bay leaves and seasoning.
2. Close the lid and cook on low for 5–6 hrs until the vegetables are tender and the sauce has thickened. Check the seasoning and stir in lemon juice to taste. Serve with crusty bread, if you like.
3. Once cooled, the casserole will keep frozen in an airtight container for up to three months. Defrost thoroughly in the fridge and reheat until piping hot.

NUTRITIONAL INFO

PER SERVING KCAL **333** | FAT **9G** | SATURATES **1G** | CARBS **44G** | SUGARS **13G** | FIBRE **15G** | PROTEIN **13G** | SALT **0.5G**

Chilli Con Carne

Prep: 25 mins
Cook: 6 hrs and 30 mins–8 hrs and 30 mins

Serves 6–8

3 tbsp olive oil
500g (1lb 2oz) minced beef
1 onion, finely chopped
1 celery stick, finely chopped
1 large red pepper, thickly sliced
2 garlic cloves, crushed
2 tsp ground cumin
1 tsp smoked paprika
2 tsp dried oregano
2–3 tbsp chipotle paste
3 tbsp tomato purée
400g (14oz) can chopped tomatoes
400ml (14fl oz) beef stock
2 × 400g (14oz) cans black beans, drained and rinsed
4 small squares of dark chocolate (70% cocoa solids)

To serve

rice
tortilla chips
lime wedges

1 Heat 1½ tbsp oil in a large, nonstick pan over a high heat and fry the minced beef for 10–12 mins or until evenly browned. Tip into your slow cooker.

2 Heat the remaining oil in the pan. Fry the onion, celery and red pepper for 10 mins or until softened. Add the garlic, cumin and paprika and fry for 1 min. Tip into the slow cooker.

3 Stir in the oregano, chipotle paste, tomato purée, tomatoes and stock. Season. Cover and cook on low for 6–8 hrs. Stir in the beans and chocolate during the final 30 mins of cooking.

4 Serve with a bowl of rice, some tortilla chips and lime wedges for squeezing over.

5 Once cooled, the chilli will keep frozen in an airtight container for up to two months. Defrost thoroughly in the fridge and reheat until piping hot.

NUTRITIONAL INFO

PER SERVING (IF SERVING 8) KCAL **342** | FAT **20G** | SATURATES **7G** | CARBS **17G** | SUGARS **7G** | FIBRE **7G** | PROTEIN **20G** | SALT **0.48G**

Comforting Beef Goulash

Prep: 25 mins
Cook: 6 hrs and 30 mins – 7 hrs and 30 mins

Serves 8

3 tbsp olive oil
2kg (4lb 8oz) braising or stewing steak, cut into chunks
2 large onions, finely chopped
4 mixed peppers, cut into 4cm (1½ inch) chunks
3 garlic cloves, crushed
2 tbsp plain flour
2 tsp caraway seeds
2 tsp hot smoked paprika
1 tbsp sweet smoked paprika, plus extra to serve
4 tbsp tomato purée
4 large tomatoes, chopped
400–500ml (14–18fl oz) beef stock
300ml (10fl oz) soured cream
small bunch of parsley, chopped
small roasted potatoes, to serve (optional)

1 Heat 2 tbsp oil in a deep frying pan over a medium heat. Season and sear the beef in batches until brown on all sides. Transfer to a plate.

2 Put the remaining oil in the pan and fry the onions for 10 mins until lightly golden. Add the peppers and garlic and fry for another 5–10 mins, then stir in the flour and all of the spices. Cook for 2 mins more, then stir in the tomato purée, tomatoes and 400ml (14fl oz) beef stock. Season well. Bring the mixture to a simmer, then tip into your slow cooker with the seared beef. Add the remaining stock, if needed, to cover the meat completely. Cover and cook on low for 6–7 hrs until the beef is tender and the sauce has thickened slightly. At this stage, once cooled, the goulash will keep frozen in an airtight container for up to two months. Defrost thoroughly in the fridge and reheat until piping hot, then serve as below.

3 Season to taste, then swirl the soured cream and most of the parsley through the stew. Scatter over the remaining parsley and some sweet smoked paprika, then serve with small roasted potatoes, if you like.

NUTRITIONAL INFO

PER SERVING KCAL **528** | FAT **28G** | SATURATES **12G** | CARBS **14G** | SUGARS **10G** | FIBRE **5G** | PROTEIN **52G** | SALT **0.3G**

Beef Stroganoff

Prep: 20 mins
Cook: 5 hrs and 30 mins–8 hrs and 30 mins

Serves 4

750g (1lb 10oz) stewing steak, cut into strips
1 tbsp vegetable or rapeseed oil, plus extra if needed
2 onions, sliced
2 garlic cloves, crushed
1 beef stock cube
1 tbsp Dijon mustard
50g (1¾oz) butter
200g (7oz) chestnut mushrooms, halved
2 tsp cornflour
200ml (7fl oz) soured cream
small bunch of parsley, chopped
paprika, to garnish
tagliatelle or mashed potato, to serve

1 Season the beef. Heat the oil in a wide frying pan and add the beef in batches so as not to overcrowd the pan. Cook over a high heat until deep brown, then transfer to your slow cooker. Add the onions and garlic to the pan and cook for a few minutes until soft, adding more oil, if needed. Add a splash of water and scrape any bits from the bottom of the pan. Tip everything into the slow cooker.

2 Add the stock cube to the beef, then the mustard and season. Add enough water to just cover the beef, put the lid on and cook on high for 5–6 hrs or low for 6–8 hrs.

3 About 30 mins before serving, melt the butter in a frying pan and cook the mushrooms until soft and caramelized. Tip into the slow cooker. Mix the cornflour with a dash of water in the frying pan, then add about 100ml (3½fl oz) more water and bring to a simmer. Once thickened, pour into the slow cooker with the soured cream and stir in. Turn to high (if not already) and cook for another 20 mins. Stir through the parsley, reserving a little for a garnish. Serve with tagliatelle or mashed potato, garnished with the remaining parsley and a pinch of paprika.

NUTRITIONAL INFO

PER SERVING KCAL **988** | FAT **61G** | SATURATES **28G** | CARBS **76G** | SUGARS **11G** | FIBRE **7G** | PROTEIN **31G** | SALT **1.2G**

Sausage Cassoulet

Prep: 15 mins
Cook: 6 hrs and 25 mins–8 hrs and 25 mins

Serves 6

1 tbsp vegetable oil
12 Toulouse-style sausages
200g (7oz) bacon lardons
2 onions, finely chopped
2 celery sticks, finely chopped
2 garlic cloves, crushed
1 tbsp smoked paprika
½ bunch of thyme, leaves picked and roughly chopped
200ml (7fl oz) white wine
400g (14oz) can chopped tomatoes
200ml (7fl oz) chicken or vegetable stock
400g (14oz) can butter beans, drained and rinsed
400g (14oz) can haricot beans, drained and rinsed
1 tbsp golden caster sugar
1 tbsp red wine vinegar
crusty bread, to serve (optional)

1 Heat the oil in a large frying pan over a high heat and brown the sausages all over – you don't have to cook them all the way through. Set aside on a plate. Add the lardons, onions and celery to the pan and cook over a medium heat for 8–10 mins until the onion is translucent and the lardons crisp. Stir in the garlic, paprika and thyme and fry for 3 mins.

2 Pour in the wine and simmer for 5–10 mins until reduced by half. Tip in the chopped tomatoes, stock, both lots of beans, the sugar and vinegar. Stir until combined and bring to the boil. Pour into your slow cooker (ours had a 5 litre/8¾ pint capacity) with the sausages. Cover and cook on low for 6–8 hrs. Serve with crusty bread.

NUTRITIONAL INFO

PER SERVING KCAL **501** | FAT **29G** | SATURATES **9G** | CARBS **27G** | SUGARS **11G** | FIBRE **10G** | PROTEIN **24G** | SALT **2.5G**

Cholent

Prep: 30 mins
Cook: 10 hrs and 30 mins–12 hrs and 30 mins

Serves 6

2 tbsp sunflower oil
1 large onion, roughly chopped
6 garlic cloves, finely chopped
1 tbsp golden caster sugar
1.2kg (2lb 10oz) beef brisket, cut into 2.5cm (1 inch) cubes
450g (1lb) potatoes, peeled and cut into large chunks
250g (9oz) sweet potato, peeled and cut into large chunks
2 parsnips, peeled and cut into chunks
225g (8oz) carrots, peeled and cut into chunks
400g (14oz) can butter beans, drained and rinsed
400g (14oz) can chickpeas, drained and rinsed
150g (5½oz) pearl barley
2 tbsp date syrup or honey
1 tsp sweet smoked paprika
1 tsp smoked paprika
2 tbsp tomato purée
1 tsp onion granules

1 Heat 1 tbsp oil in a large frying pan over a medium–high heat and cook the onion, stirring frequently, for 8–10 mins until soft and translucent. Add the garlic and cook for a few minutes until soft and fragrant. Sprinkle over the sugar and continue to cook for 2–3 mins, stirring frequently, until golden. Tip onto a plate and set aside.

2 Wipe the pan with kitchen paper and add the remaining oil. Season the cubed brisket well and cook over a high heat in batches for 5–10 mins, until browned on all sides. Transfer the browned beef to a second plate or bowl.

3 Now, layer up the ingredients in your slow cooker. First add the vegetables (including the cooked onion) in the base, then the beans, chickpeas and barley (give the dish a shake so that they fall into the gaps) and finally the browned beef.

4 Pour 250ml (9fl oz) water into a large jug and stir in the remaining ingredients with 3 tsp salt, plus a good grinding of black pepper. Whisk well to combine. Pour over the beef and vegetables, then top up with enough water (about 1.5 litres/2⅔ pints) to just cover the contents – do not stir.

5 Cover and cook on low for 10–12 hrs until the meat and vegetables are tender. Check the seasoning, then serve piping hot.

NUTRITIONAL INFO

PER SERVING KCAL **746** | FAT **29G** | SATURATES **10G** | CARBS **69G** | SUGARS **19G** | FIBRE **12G** | PROTEIN **47G** | SALT **2.69G**

Pork Casserole

Prep: 15 mins
Cook: 5 hrs and 20 mins–8 hrs and 20 mins

Serves 4

1 tbsp vegetable or rapeseed oil
750g (1lb 10oz) boneless pork shoulder, cut into large chunks
1 onion, chopped
1 leek, chopped
1 carrot, chopped
1 bouquet garni (we used 2 bay leaves, 3 sage leaves and 4 thyme sprigs)
1 chicken stock cube
2 tsp Dijon mustard, plus extra to serve
1 tbsp apple cider vinegar
2 tsp cornflour
1 tbsp honey
thyme leaves, to garnish
mashed potato, to serve

1 Heat the oil in a wide frying pan over a high heat. Season the pork, then add to the hot pan in batches. Cook until deep brown all over, then transfer to your slow cooker. Add the onion and leek to the frying pan and cook for a few minutes until they soften. Add a splash of water and scrape any tasty bits from the bottom, then tip everything into the slow cooker. Add the carrot, bouquet garni, stock cube, mustard and vinegar, season and add enough water to just cover the ingredients. Stir, then cover and cook on high for 5–6 hrs or low for 6–8 hrs.

2 In a saucepan, mix the cornflour and honey with 1–2 tsp of the liquid from the slow cooker to make a smooth paste. Add another 100ml (3½fl oz) of the liquid and bring to a simmer until thickened, then stir back into the casserole. Scatter with thyme leaves and serve with mashed potato and extra mustard.

NUTRITIONAL INFO

PER SERVING KCAL **416** | FAT **21G** | SATURATES **6G** | CARBS **13G** | SUGARS **10G** | FIBRE **4G** | PROTEIN **41G** | SALT **1.2G**

Puttanesca Squid

Prep: 20 mins
Cook: 3 hrs and 10 mins

Serves 4

2 tsp olive oil
1 onion, finely chopped
3 garlic cloves, crushed
6 canned anchovy fillets
large pinch of chilli flakes (optional)
1 tsp dried oregano
400g (14oz) can cherry tomatoes or chopped tomatoes
600g (1lb 5oz) prepared squid, tubes cut into rings
3 tbsp capers, drained
150g (5½oz) pitted black olives
125ml (4fl oz) white wine
small handful of parsley, finely chopped
crusty bread, to serve

TIP

You can buy pre-prepared squid from your local fishmonger or fish counter.

1 Heat the oil in a frying pan over a medium heat and fry the onion for 6–8 mins until soft and beginning to brown. Add the garlic and anchovies and cook for 1 min more before scattering in the chilli, if using, and the oregano. Cook for 30 seconds, then tip into your slow cooker.

2 Add the tomatoes, squid, capers and olives. Pour in the white wine and give everything a good stir. Cover and cook on high for 3 hrs until the sauce has thickened a little (it will be soup-like). Serve in bowls with the chopped parsley scattered over and some crusty bread for dunking.

NUTRITIONAL INFO

PER SERVING KCAL **310** | FAT **15G** | SATURATES **2G** | CARBS **10G** | SUGARS **7G** | FIBRE **3G** | PROTEIN **27G** | SALT **2.6G**

Lamb Tagine

Prep: 20 mins
Cook: 4 hrs and 20 mins–8 hrs and 20 mins

Serves 4

1 tbsp olive oil
900g (2lb) boneless lamb shoulder, neck or leg, cut into chunks
1 onion, chopped
3 carrots, cut into chunks
2 tsp ras el hanout
1 tsp ground cumin
1 tbsp tomato purée
1 chicken or lamb stock cube
1 sweet potato, peeled and cut into chunks
30g (1oz) dried cherries
½ tsp honey
bunch of coriander, chopped
couscous, to serve

1 Heat the oil in a frying pan and fry the lamb in batches until browned all over. Tip it into your slow cooker. Fry the onion in the same pan for 5 mins or until it softens a little. Add the carrots and spices and stir everything together, then add the tomato purée, stock cube and 250ml (9fl oz) water, and swirl everything around the pan. Tip into the slow cooker. Add the sweet potato, dried cherries, honey and another 500ml (18fl oz) water and stir well.

2 Cover and cook on high for 4 hrs or low for 8 hrs. Scatter with the coriander and serve with couscous.

NUTRITIONAL INFO

PER SERVING KCAL **649** | FAT **45G** | SATURATES **20G** | CARBS **17G** | SUGARS **10G** | FIBRE **5G** | PROTEIN **42G** | SALT **1.3G**

Better-Than-Baked Beans with Spicy Wedges

Prep: 10 mins
Cook: 9 hrs and 5 mins–10 hrs and 10 mins

Serves 2

1 tsp oil

1 onion, thinly sliced

2 streaky bacon rashers, coarsely chopped

1 tsp sugar (any kind)

400g (14oz) can chopped tomatoes

200ml (7fl oz) chicken stock

400g (14oz) can cannellini, butter or haricot beans in water, drained

For the wedges

1 tbsp white flour (plain or self-raising)

½ tsp cayenne pepper, paprika or mild chilli powder

1 tsp dried mixed herbs (optional)

2 small baking potatoes, each cut into 8 wedges

2 tsp olive or vegetable oil

1 Heat the oil in a nonstick frying pan, then gently fry the onion and bacon for 5–10 mins until softened and just starting to turn golden. Add the sugar, tomatoes, stock and some seasoning, then transfer to your slow cooker and stir in the beans. Cover and cook on low overnight or for 9–10 hrs.

2 Towards the end of the cooking time, make the potato wedges. Heat the oven to 200°C/180°C fan/400°F/Gas Mark 6. Mix together the flour, spice, herbs, if using, and some salt and pepper, then toss with the potatoes and oil until well coated. Tip into a roasting tin and bake for about 35 mins until crisp and cooked through.

3 Serve the beans with the potato wedges.

NUTRITIONAL INFO

PER SERVING KCAL **438** | FAT **11G** | SATURATES **3G** | CARBS **59G** | SUGARS **16G** | FIBRE **14G** | PROTEIN **20G** | SALT **1.25G**

Set & Forget

✳

Simple Lamb Madras

Prep: 10 mins, plus chilling
Cook: 6 hrs

Serves 2

1 large onion, sliced
3 tbsp Madras curry paste
400g (14oz) can chopped tomatoes
2 tsp vegetable bouillon powder
25g (1oz) dried red lentils, rinsed
210g (7½oz) can chickpeas
1 tbsp grated ginger
1 tsp cumin seeds
1 cinnamon stick
75g (2¾oz) curly kale, chopped
240g (8½oz) lean lamb, cut into chunks

To serve
brown rice
chutney

1 Put all the ingredients into your slow cooker, fill the tomato can one-third full with water, add to the pot and stir well. Cover with the lid and chill in the fridge overnight.

2 The next day, stir again, then cook on low for 6 hrs until the lamb and vegetables are tender. Serve with brown rice and chutney.

3 Once cooled, the madras will keep frozen in an airtight container for up to two months. Defrost thoroughly in the fridge and reheat until piping hot.

NUTRITIONAL INFO

PER SERVING KCAL **568** | FAT **19G** | SATURATES **5G** | CARBS **49G** | SUGARS **17G** | FIBRE **13G** | PROTEIN **43G** | SALT **1.3G**

Mexican Barbacoa

Prep: 15 mins
Cook: 7 hrs

Serves 4

4 tomatoes, quartered
2 dried ancho chillies, deseeded
1 tsp dried oregano
1 tsp cumin seeds
1 garlic bulb, cloves peeled
400ml (14fl oz) red wine
½ bone-in lamb shoulder (about 1.25kg/2lb 12oz)
50g (1¾oz) dark chocolate (70% cocoa solids), broken into squares
1 cinnamon stick
8 large new potatoes (about 450g/1lb)
coriander, to garnish

For the slaw

juice of 1 orange
1 tbsp white wine vinegar
1 red chilli, deseeded and finely chopped (optional)
1 red onion, thinly sliced
300g (10½oz) shredded white cabbage
150g (5½oz) radishes, thinly sliced
generous handful chopped coriander

TIP

If you have trouble getting the seeds out of the dried chillies, pour boiling water over them and leave for 1–2 mins – they will quickly soften enough to cut them open.

1 First make the white cabbage and radish slaw. Mix the orange juice, vinegar, chilli, if using, and onion in a large bowl, and mix with a little salt. Add the cabbage, radishes and and coriander and toss really well. Cover and chill until needed.

2 Put the tomatoes, chillies, oregano, cumin and garlic in a food processor with one-third of the wine, add 1 tsp salt and blitz until smooth.

3 Put the lamb in your slow cooker pot (we used a 6.5 litre/11½ pint model). Pour over the chilli mix, then add the rest of the wine with the chocolate, cinnamon stick and whole potatoes. Cover and cook on low for 7 hrs until the lamb is really tender but the potatoes are still firm.

4 To serve, remove the bones and skin from the lamb and pull the meat apart into large chunks. Chop the potatoes into chunks and skim the fat from the cooking juices. Serve the lamb, potatoes and juices in bowls garnished with coriander, with the white cabbage and radish slaw on top.

NUTRITIONAL INFO

PER SERVING KCAL **800** | FAT **43G** | SATURATES **21G** | CARBS **32G** | SUGARS **15G** | FIBRE **9G** | PROTEIN **47G** | SALT **1.6G**

Full-of-Flavour Roast Chicken

Prep: 15 mins
Cook: 5 hrs and 30 mins–6 hours and 30 mins

Serves 4

1 large onion, thickly sliced
2 carrots, halved lengthways and chopped
1 small or medium chicken
2 tbsp butter, softened
1 bay leaf

1 Put the onion and carrots in the base of your slow cooker pot to form a protective layer to sit the chicken on and add 100ml (3½fl oz) boiling water. Gently ease the chicken skin away from the breast. Stir some salt and pepper into the butter, then push the butter under the skin in an even layer. Put the bay leaf in the cavity of the chicken and sit it on top of the onion and carrots.

2 Cover and cook on low for 5 hrs, then check that the chicken is cooked by wiggling the wing – it should feel very loose. Tip the chicken up so that any juices inside flow out, then cook on high for 30 mins. If the chicken isn't cooked through after the initial time, cook for another hour, then turn the heat up. If you want the skin to be browned, transfer it to a roasting tin and grill it for a couple of minutes.

3 There will be some juices in the base of the dish with the veg. Tip the contents of the pot through a sieve and press the veg gently to make sure you get every last drop. Serve the pan juices with the chicken, with the veg on the side, if you like.

NUTRITIONAL INFO

PER SERVING KCAL **400** | FAT **25G** | SATURATES **9G** | CARBS **2G** | SUGARS **1G** | FIBRE **1G** | PROTEIN **41G** | SALT **0.5G**

✳

Prep: 20 mins
Cook: 5–8 hrs

Coconut Chicken Curry

Serves 4–6

1 red onion, finely chopped
8 boneless, skinless chicken thighs, cut into chunks
4 garlic cloves, crushed
thumb-sized piece of ginger, peeled and finely grated
6 tbsp curry paste
400ml (14fl oz) coconut milk
400g (14oz) can chopped tomatoes
500g (1lb 2oz) sweet potatoes or butternut squash, peeled, deseeded and roughly chopped
1 red chilli, sliced, to garnish (optional)

To serve

coriander
rice
naan

1 Tip all the ingredients, except the chilli, into your slow cooker and stir to combine. Cover and cook on high for 5 hrs or on low for 8 hrs until the chicken is tender and cooked through, removing the lid for the final hour to thicken the sauce.

2 Garnish with the red chilli, if you like, and serve with coriander, rice and naan.

3 Once cooled, the curry will keep frozen in an airtight container for up to two months. Defrost thoroughly in the fridge and reheat until piping hot.

NUTRITIONAL INFO

PER SERVING (IF SERVING 6) KCAL **384** | FAT **22G** | SATURATES **11G** | CARBS **25G** | SUGARS **10G** | FIBRE **5G** | PROTEIN **19G** | SALT **0.72G**

White Chicken Chilli

Prep: 15 mins
Cook: 4–5 hrs

Serves 4

300g (10½oz) tomatillo salsa
2 tbsp pickled jalapeños, chopped
4 garlic cloves, crushed
1 tsp dried oregano
2 tsp ground coriander
2 tsp ground cumin
handful of coriander, leaves picked, stalks finely chopped
4 spring onions, sliced
400g (14oz) can white beans, drained and rinsed
2 green peppers, roughly chopped
zest of ½ lime
200ml (7fl oz) hot chicken stock
4 skinless chicken breasts

To serve

soured cream
grated cheddar
rice
lime wedges
tortilla chips

1 Tip all the ingredients, except the coriander leaves, into your slow cooker. Season and mix well, making sure the chicken is submerged. Cover and cook on high for 4–5 hrs.

2 Remove the chicken to a board and shred using two forks. Roughly mash half the bean mixture using a potato masher, leaving the rest chunky. Return the chicken to the slow cooker and season.

3 Top with the coriander leaves and serve with soured cream, grated cheddar, rice, lime wedges for squeezing over and tortilla chips.

NUTRITIONAL INFO

PER SERVING KCAL **360** | FAT **12G** | SATURATES **3G** | CARBS **17G** | SUGARS **7G** | FIBRE **7G** | PROTEIN **42G** | SALT **2G**

✳

Prep: 20 mins
Cook: 3 hrs and 30 mins–8 hrs

Christmas Leftovers Turkey Curry

Serves 6–8

1 onion, chopped
4 garlic cloves, crushed
thumb-sized piece of ginger, peeled and finely grated
1 red pepper, chopped
350g (12oz) sweet potatoes, carrots, parsnips or leftover roast veg, peeled and chopped where necessary
700g (1lb 9oz) cooked or raw turkey, cut into large pieces
400g (14oz) can chickpeas, drained and rinsed
2 tbsp balti curry paste
1 tbsp tomato purée
400g (14oz) can chopped tomatoes
400g (14oz) can coconut milk
small bunch of coriander, leaves picked, stalks finely chopped
120g (4¼oz) spinach (optional)
rice, to serve

1 Tip the onion, garlic, ginger, red pepper, sweet potatoes and vegetables, turkey and chickpeas into your slow cooker. Stir in the curry paste and tomato purée, ensuring everything is well coated. Pour in the chopped tomatoes and coconut milk and scatter in the chopped coriander stalks, 1 tsp salt and some ground black pepper. Mix everything to combine. Cover and cook on high for 3 hrs 30 mins or on low for 8 hrs. If you want to add spinach, tip it in 15 mins before the end of the cooking time. Stir well after 5 mins, once it has started to wilt.

2 Serve the turkey curry with rice, scattered with the coriander leaves.

3 Once cooled, the curry will keep frozen in an airtight container for up to two months. Defrost thoroughly in the fridge and reheat until piping hot.

NUTRITIONAL INFO

PER SERVING (IF SERVING 8) KCAL **289** | FAT **12G** | SATURATES **8G** | CARBS **19G** | SUGARS **10G** | FIBRE **5G** | PROTEIN **25G** | SALT **1G**

Turkey Casserole

Prep: 15 mins
Cook: 3 hrs and 30 mins–8 hrs

Serves 6–8

1 onion, chopped
2 carrots, roughly chopped
1 leek, sliced
½ swede, peeled and roughly chopped
2 parsnips, peeled and roughly chopped
700g (1lb 9oz) turkey, cut into large pieces (or use the same amount of leftover roasted turkey)
2 tbsp plain flour
½ small bunch of sage, leaves picked and chopped
2 bay leaves
2 tbsp wholegrain mustard
2 tbsp tomato purée
1.5 litres (2⅔ pints) turkey or chicken stock
griddled bread or cooked potatoes, to serve

TIP

Cut the vegetables into even-sized pieces so they cook in similar amounts of time.

1. Tip the onion, carrots, leek, swede, parsnips and turkey into your slow cooker. Sprinkle over the flour, then mix to combine everything.
2. Add the sage, bay leaves, mustard and tomato purée and mix well. Pour in the stock, season well and give everything a quick stir. Cover and cook on high for 3 hrs 30 mins or on low for 8 hrs.
3. Serve with griddled bread or cooked potatoes.
4. Once cooled, the casserole will keep frozen in an airtight container for up to two months. Defrost thoroughly in the fridge and reheat until piping hot.

NUTRITIONAL INFO

PER SERVING (IF SERVING 8) KCAL **206** | FAT **3G** | SATURATES **1G** | CARBS **15G** | SUGARS **7G** | FIBRE **6G** | PROTEIN **27G** | SALT **1.5G**

V

Prep: 15 mins
Cook: 6–8 hrs

Summer Aubergines

Serves 6

- 4 tbsp olive oil
- 1 red onion, sliced
- 2 garlic cloves, crushed
- 500g (1lb 2oz) aubergines, cut into 1cm (½ inch) thick slices
- 300g (10½oz) ripe tomatoes, quartered
- 1 small fennel bulb, sliced
- 50g (1¾oz) sundried tomatoes
- 1 tsp coriander seeds
- crusty bread, to serve

For the dressing

- small bunch of flat leaf parsley, roughly chopped
- small bunch of basil, roughly chopped
- small bunch of chives, roughly chopped
- 2 tbsp olive oil
- juice of 1 lemon
- 2 tsp capers

For the topping

- 100g (3½oz) feta cheese, crumbled
- 50g (1¾oz) toasted flaked almonds

1 Pour 2 tbsp olive oil into your slow cooker and put the onion and crushed garlic on top. Brush the aubergines with the remaining olive oil. Put them into the slow cooker on top of the onion and nestle the tomatoes, fennel slices and sundried tomatoes in and around the aubergines. Sprinkle the coriander seeds over the top, then season everything well with salt and pepper. Cover and cook on low for 6–8 hrs or until the aubergines are soft.

2 Put all the dressing ingredients into the bowl of a mini food processor and blitz until smooth.

3 Pour the herby dressing over the aubergine mixture, top with the feta and toasted flaked almonds and serve with some crusty bread on the side.

NUTRITIONAL INFO

PER SERVING KCAL **269** | FAT **20G** | SATURATES **4G** | CARBS **11G** | SUGARS **9G** | FIBRE **6G** | PROTEIN **8G** | SALT **0.6G**

V Ve

Prep: 10 mins, plus chilling
Cook: 6 hrs

Creamy Vegetable Curry

Serves 2

400ml (14fl oz) light coconut milk
3 tbsp mild curry paste
2 tsp vegetable bouillon powder
1 red chilli, deseeded and sliced
1 tbsp finely chopped ginger
3 garlic cloves, sliced
200g (7oz) butternut squash or sweet potato, peeled, deseeded and cut into chunks
1 red pepper, sliced
1 small aubergine, halved and thickly sliced
15g (½oz) coriander, chopped
160g (5¾oz) frozen peas, defrosted
juice of 1 lime, to taste
wholemeal flatbreads, to serve

1 Put the coconut milk, curry paste, bouillon powder, chilli, ginger, garlic, butternut squash or sweet potato, red pepper and aubergine into your slow cooker and stir well. Cover with the lid and chill overnight.

2 Cook on low for 6 hrs until the vegetables are really tender, then stir in the coriander and defrosted peas. The heat of the curry should be enough to warm them through. Taste and add a good squeeze of lime juice for extra zing. Serve with wholemeal flatbreads.

NUTRITIONAL INFO

PER SERVING KCAL **399** | FAT **22G** | SATURATES **13G** | CARBS **31G** | SUGARS **18G** | FIBRE **14G** | PROTEIN **11G** | SALT **2.02G**

V

Velvety Mac 'n' Cheese

Prep: 15 mins
Cook: 1 hr and 30 mins

Serves 4

350g (12oz) macaroni
600ml (20fl oz) whole milk, plus extra if needed
50g (1¾oz) butter, cut into small cubes
50g (¾oz) soft cheese
100g (3½oz) mature cheddar (or vegetarian alternative), grated, plus extra to serve
20g (¾oz) parmesan (or vegetarian alternative), plus extra to serve
crusty bread, to serve (optional)

1 Pour boiling water over the pasta and drain, then put everything in your slow cooker and stir well. Season, cover and cook on low for 1 hr. Stir again, put the lid back on and cook for another 30 mins until the pasta is cooked and the sauce has reduced enough to coat it.

2 Leave the lid off and reduce for the last 10 mins if you need to, or add a splash more milk if it's too dry. Serve with extra cheese and some crusty bread, if you like.

NUTRITIONAL INFO

PER SERVING KCAL **666** | FAT **31G** | SATURATES **19G** | CARBS **71G** | SUGARS **9G** | FIBRE **4G** | PROTEIN **25G** | SALT **1G**

✳ V

Prep: 5 mins
Cook: 4 hrs

Simple Sweet-and-Sour Red Cabbage

Serves 6

1 red cabbage (about 1kg/2lb 4oz), quartered and finely shredded
½ tsp ground mixed spice
50g (1¾oz) light brown soft sugar
5 tbsp red wine vinegar
large knob of butter

1 Tip the cabbage into your slow cooker, then scatter in the mixed spice, sugar and some salt and pepper. Pour in the vinegar and stir well, then dot over the butter. Put the lid on and cook on low for 3 hrs 30 mins until starting to soften.

2 Remove the lid and cook for another 30 mins until the cabbage is very tender and sticky and the liquid has reduced. Taste for seasoning and then serve.

3 Once cool, the cabbage will keep covered in the fridge for up to three days or frozen for up to two months. Defrost thoroughly in the fridge and reheat in the slow cooker or in a saucepan over a medium heat until piping hot.

NUTRITIONAL INFO

PER SERVING KCAL **90** | FAT **2G** | SATURATES **1G** | CARBS **14G** | SUGARS **13G** | FIBRE **5G** | PROTEIN **2G** | SALT **0.1G**

Comfort Food

V Ve

Prep: 10 mins
Cook: 5 hrs and 10 mins

Protein-Rich Breakfast Beans

Serves 4

1 tbsp olive oil
1 onion, thinly sliced
2 garlic cloves, chopped
1 tbsp white or red wine vinegar
1 heaped tbsp light brown soft sugar
400g (14oz) can pinto beans, drained and rinsed
200ml (7fl oz) passata
small bunch of coriander, chopped
toast, to serve

1. Heat the oil in a large frying pan and fry the onion until it starts to brown, then add the garlic and cook for 1 min. Add the vinegar and sugar and bubble for 1 min. Stir in the beans and passata and season with black pepper. Tip everything into your slow cooker.
2. Cover and cook on low for 5 hrs. If the sauce seems a little thin, turn the heat to high and cook for a few more minutes. Stir through the coriander before serving with toast.

NUTRITIONAL INFO

PER SERVING KCAL **149** | FAT **3G** | SATURATES **0.5G** | CARBS **21G** | SUGARS **12G** | FIBRE **5G** | PROTEIN **6G** | SALT **0.39G**

V

Turkish Breakfast Eggs

Prep: 15 mins
Cook: 5 hrs and 10 mins–6 hrs and 10 mins

Serves 4

1 tbsp olive oil, plus extra for oiling
2 onions, finely sliced
1 red pepper, finely sliced
1 small red chilli, finely sliced
8 cherry tomatoes
1 slice of sourdough bread, cubed
4 eggs
2 tbsp skimmed milk
small bunch of parsley, finely chopped
4 tbsp natural yogurt, to serve

1 Oil the inside of your slow cooker. Heat the olive oil in a heavy-based frying pan. Stir in the onions, red pepper and chilli and cook until they begin to soften. Tip into the slow cooker, add the cherry tomatoes and bread and stir well. Season.

2 Whisk the eggs with the milk and parsley, then pour over the top, making sure all the other ingredients are covered. Cover and cook on low for 5–6 hrs until set. Serve with the yogurt.

NUTRITIONAL INFO
PER SERVING KCAL **165** | FAT **8G** | SATURATES **2G** | CARBS **13G** | SUGARS **7G** | FIBRE **3G** | PROTEIN **9G** | SALT **0.32G**

Beef Pie

Prep: 30 mins, plus chilling
Cook: 5–9 hrs

Serves 6

500ml (18fl oz) hot beef stock
1 tbsp Worcestershire sauce
2 tbsp tomato purée
2 tbsp cornflour
2 tbsp vegetable oil
1kg (2lb 4oz) braising or stewing steak, cut into chunks
2 onions, finely chopped
2 carrots, finely chopped
1 celery stick, finely chopped
2 thyme or rosemary sprigs
green vegetables, to serve

For the pastry

225g (8oz) plain flour, plus extra for dusting
170g (6oz) unsalted butter, chilled and cut into small cubes
1 egg, beaten with a pinch of salt

1 Pour the stock into your slow cooker and turn to high. Mix together the Worcestershire sauce, tomato purée and cornflour, then whisk into the stock.

2 Heat 1 tbsp oil in a large pan and fry the beef in batches over a high heat until browned. Transfer to the slow cooker. Add the remaining oil to the pan, lower the heat slightly and fry the onions, carrots and celery with some seasoning for 10 mins until golden. Add to the slow cooker along with the thyme or rosemary. Cover and cook on high for 4 hrs or on low for 8 hrs until the beef is very tender. Leave to cool, then keep chilled for up to 24 hrs until needed.

3 To make the flaky pastry, put the flour, ½ tsp fine salt and the butter in a large bowl. Add 115ml (3¾fl oz) very cold water and, using a round-bladed knife, bring together into a rough dough. Cover and chill for 30 mins.

4 On a lightly floured work surface, roll the dough out into a 1cm (½ inch) thick rectangle that is three times as long as it is wide. Fold the top third of the pastry down and the bottom third up over the top to create a block. Turn 90 degrees and roll out to the same size rectangle as before, then fold in the same way again. Cover and chill for 30 mins.

5 Repeat the rolling and folding four times, then wrap and chill for at least 30 mins until ready to use.

6 Heat the oven to 200°C/180°C fan/400°F/Gas Mark 6. Spoon the pie filling into an ovenproof dish, then roll the pastry out until large enough to cover the dish. Brush the rim with some of the egg, then lay the pastry over the top. Trim the overhanging pastry, then crimp the edges. Brush with the remaining egg and make a couple of slits for the air to escape, then put the dish on a baking tray and bake for 40–45 mins until puffed and dark golden. Leave to cool a little before serving with some green vegetables.

NUTRITIONAL INFO

PER SERVING KCAL **678** | FAT **39G** | SATURATES **19G** | CARBS **41G** | SUGARS **7G** | FIBRE **5G** | PROTEIN **38G** | SALT **0.88G**

Mince & Tatties

✳

Prep: 20 mins
Cook: 3 hrs and 30 mins–6 hrs and 30 mins

Serves 4

1 tbsp sunflower oil
500g (1lb 2oz) minced beef
1 onion, chopped
1 large carrot, chopped
1 tbsp plain flour
1 tbsp tomato ketchup or tomato purée (optional)
1 tbsp Worcestershire sauce
500ml (18fl oz) beef stock

For the tatties

800g (1lb 12oz) Maris Piper, King Edward or other floury potatoes, peeled and chopped
100ml (3½fl oz) milk
25g (1oz) butter

1 Heat the oil in a large pan, crumble in the minced beef and stir to coat in the oil. Cook for 15 mins, stirring occasionally, until the beef is browned and the fat from the meat has been released. Stir in the onion and carrot and cook for 10 mins until they soften and start to turn brown.

2 Sprinkle over the flour and cook for a further 2 mins. Stir in the ketchup or tomato purée, if using, and splash in the Worcestershire sauce, then gradually stir in the stock. Season and tip into your slow cooker. Cover and cook on high for 3–4 hrs or on low for 5–6 hrs, removing the lid for the last hour of cooking, until you have tender mince in a rich gravy. At this stage, once cooled, the mince will keep frozen in an airtight container for up to two months. Defrost thoroughly in the fridge and reheat until piping hot.

3 While the mince is cooking, make the tatties. Tip the potatoes into a pan and cover in salted cold water. Bring to the boil, then simmer for about 15 mins until tender. Drain well and allow to steam-dry for a few minutes. Mash well with the milk and butter, then season with salt and pepper. Serve the stewed mince spooned over the tatties.

NUTRITIONAL INFO

PER SERVING KCAL **504** | FAT **23G** | SATURATES **10G** | CARBS **41G** | SUGARS **8G** | FIBRE **5G** | PROTEIN **30G** | SALT **0.88G**

Rich & Tasty Lasagne

Prep: 40 mins
Cook: 3 hrs and 35 mins

Serves 4

2 tsp rapeseed oil
2 onions, finely chopped
4 celery sticks, finely chopped
4 carrots, finely chopped
2 garlic cloves, chopped
400g (14oz) lean minced beef
400g (14oz) can chopped tomatoes
2 tbsp tomato purée
2 tsp vegetable bouillon powder
1 tbsp balsamic vinegar
1 tbsp thyme leaves
6 wholewheat lasagne sheets
salad, to serve

For the sauce

400ml (14fl oz) whole milk
50g (1¾oz) wholemeal flour
1 bay leaf
generous grating of nutmeg
15g (½oz) parmesan, finely grated

1 Heat the oil in a large nonstick pan and fry the onions, celery, carrots and garlic for 5–10 mins, stirring frequently, until softened and starting to colour. Tip in the minced beef and break it down with a wooden spoon, stirring until it browns. Pour in the tomatoes, then fill the tomato can one-quarter full with water and add to the pan along with the tomato purée, bouillon powder, balsamic vinegar, thyme and plenty of black pepper. Return to the boil and cook for 5 mins more.

2 Spoon half the meat into your slow cooker and top with half the lasagne sheets, breaking them where necessary so that they cover as much of the meat layer as possible. Top with the rest of the meat, then another layer of the lasagne sheets. Cover and cook on low while you make the sauce.

3 Place the milk and flour in a saucepan with the bay leaf and nutmeg and cook on the hob, whisking continuously until thickened. Carry on cooking for a few minutes to cook the flour. Remove the bay leaf and stir in the cheese. Pour onto the pasta and spread out with a spatula, then cover and cook on low for 3 hrs until the meat is cooked and the pasta is tender. Allow to settle for 10 mins before serving with salad.

4 Once cooled, you can transfer the lasagne to a freezerproof, ovenproof dish and freeze for up to two months. Defrost thoroughly in the fridge and reheat in a gentle oven until piping hot.

NUTRITIONAL INFO

PER SERVING KCAL **448** | FAT **12G** | SATURATES **6G** | CARBS **46G** | SUGARS **19G** | FIBRE **9G** | PROTEIN **33G** | SALT **0.71G**

Sausage Casserole

Prep: 20 mins
Cook: 4 hrs and 15 mins–8 hrs and 15 mins

Serves 4

1–2 tbsp rapeseed oil
2 red onions, finely chopped
1 celery stick, finely chopped
4 carrots, cut into chunks
12 chipolatas, halved
1 sweet potato, peeled and cut into chunks
400g (14oz) can tomatoes
1 tbsp tomato purée or tomato and veg purée
1 thyme sprig
1 rosemary sprig
1 beef stock cube
pasta, to serve

1 Heat the oil in a frying pan and fry the onions and celery over a low heat for about 5 mins until they start to soften and cook, then spoon into your slow cooker. Fry the carrots briefly in the same pan, then add them too.

2 Next, brown the sausages all over, making sure they get a really good colour because they won't get any browner in the slow cooker. Transfer to the slow cooker and add the sweet potato and tomatoes.

3 Put the tomato purée in the frying pan, add 250ml (9fl oz) boiling water and swirl everything around to pick up every last bit of flavour, then tip into the slow cooker. Add the herbs, stock cube and some pepper. Cover and cook on high for 4 hrs or on low for 8 hrs, then serve with pasta.

4 Once cooled, the casserole will keep frozen in an airtight container for up to two months. Defrost thoroughly in the fridge and reheat until piping hot.

NUTRITIONAL INFO

PER SERVING KCAL **449** | FAT **28G** | SATURATES **8G** | CARBS **27G** | SUGARS **18G** | FIBRE **8G** | PROTEIN **17G** | SALT **1.9G**

Topside with Red Wine Gravy

Prep: 20 mins, plus chilling
Cook: 6 hrs and 30 mins

Serves 6

1 tbsp black peppercorns
1 tbsp English mustard powder
2 tbsp chopped rosemary
1 tsp celery seeds
15g (½oz) dried porcini mushrooms
4 tbsp olive or rapeseed oil
1.6kg (3lb 8oz) beef topside, cut into 12 slices
600ml (20fl oz) hot beef stock
1 large carrot, roughly chopped
1 large onion, roughly chopped
2 celery sticks, roughly chopped
2 tbsp tomato purée
200ml (7fl oz) red wine
1 tbsp cornflour (optional)

To serve
mashed potato
seasonal vegetables

1 Crush the peppercorns with the mustard, rosemary, celery seeds and a little salt using a pestle and mortar. Blitz the mushrooms to a fine powder in a food processor, then stir them into the peppercorn mixture with 2 tbsp oil and rub all over the beef. Cover and chill for at least 1 hr, but preferably overnight.

2 Pour the stock into your slow cooker. Heat the remaining oil in a large pan and brown the beef all over, then put in the slow cooker, skin side up. Fry the carrot, onion and celery in the same pan over a medium–high heat for about 10 mins. Stir in the tomato purée and wine, scraping the bits off the bottom of the pan, then add this to the slow cooker.

3 Cover and cook on low for 6 hrs, then strain the liquid into a saucepan. Keep the meat and veg covered with foil so that they stay warm. Bring the liquid to the boil, then simmer until reduced by one-third and season. For thicker gravy, mix the cornflour with 2 tbsp water and whisk into the boiling liquid. Serve the beef with the gravy, along with some mashed potato and seasonal vegetables.

NUTRITIONAL INFO
PER SERVING KCAL **690** | FAT **43G** | SATURATES **16G** | CARBS **10G** | SUGARS **4G** | FIBRE **3G** | PROTEIN **58G** | SALT **0.8G**

✳

Creamy Moussaka

Prep: 10 mins
Cook: 6 hrs and 40 mins

Serves 4

2 aubergines, sliced into 1cm (½ inch) rounds
4 tbsp olive oil, plus extra for brushing
500g (1lb 2oz) minced lamb
1 onion, finely chopped
3 garlic cloves, crushed
2 × 400g (14oz) cans chopped tomatoes
125ml (4fl oz) lamb stock
3 tbsp tomato purée
1 tsp dried oregano
1 tsp ground cinnamon
50g (1¾oz) fresh breadcrumbs
chopped parsley, to serve (optional)

For the béchamel

50g (1¾oz) butter
50g (1¾oz) plain flour
500ml (18fl oz) milk
¼ tsp grated nutmeg
70g (2½oz) parmesan, finely grated
1 egg yolk

1 Heat the oven to 220°C/200°C fan/425°F/Gas Mark 7. Arrange the aubergine rounds on a large baking tray, season and drizzle with 2 tbsp olive oil. Roast in the oven for 15–20 mins or until lightly browned.

2 Meanwhile, heat the remaining olive oil in a large pan over a medium–high heat. Add the minced lamb and brown all over for 6–7 mins, before adding the onion and garlic, then cook for 5 mins. Transfer to your slow cooker, then add the chopped tomatoes, lamb stock, tomato purée, oregano and cinnamon and season well. Cover and cook on low for 6 hrs.

3 When the ragu has 20 mins cooking time left, make the béchamel. Melt the butter in a medium saucepan over a medium heat, add the flour and cook for 1–2 mins. Slowly whisk in the milk, a little at a time, until you have a lump-free sauce. Bring to a simmer and cook for 4–5 mins until thickened. Remove from the heat, stir through the nutmeg, parmesan and egg yolk and season.

4 Heat the grill to high. Lightly brush a medium baking dish with oil. Layer in half the aubergine slices, add the ragu and top with the remaining aubergine slices. Pour over the béchamel sauce, sprinkle over the breadcrumbs and grill for 5–10 mins until browned on top. Sprinkle over a little chopped parsley, if you like.

5 Once cooled, the moussaka will keep chilled, covered, for up to three days or frozen for up to three months. Defrost thoroughly in the fridge overnight, then bake at 200°C/180°C fan/400°F/Gas Mark 6 for 45–50 mins until piping hot throughout and golden brown.

NUTRITIONAL INFO

PER SERVING KCAL **808** | FAT **51G** | SATURATES **23G** | CARBS **38G** | SUGARS **18G** | FIBRE **7G** | PROTEIN **44G** | SALT **1.06G**

Shepherd's Pie

Prep: 40 mins
Cook: 5 hrs and 15 mins

Serves 4

1 tbsp olive oil
1 onion, finely chopped
3–4 thyme sprigs
2 carrots, finely chopped
250g (9oz) lean minced lamb or beef
1 tbsp plain flour
1 tbsp tomato purée
400g (14oz) can lentils or white beans, drained
1 tsp Worcestershire sauce
green vegetables, to serve

For the topping

650g (1lb 7oz) potatoes, peeled and cut into chunks
250g (9oz) sweet potatoes, peeled and cut into chunks
2 tbsp half-fat crème fraîche

1 For the topping, cook both lots of potatoes in salted simmering water for 12–13 mins or until they are cooked through. Drain well and then mash with the crème fraîche.

2 Meanwhile, heat the oil in a large frying pan, add the onion and thyme sprigs and fry for 2–3 mins. Add the carrots and fry together, stirring occasionally, until the vegetables start to brown. Stir in the meat and fry for 1–2 mins until no longer pink. Stir in the flour and cook for another 1–2 mins. Stir in the tomato purée and lentils or beans and season with pepper and the Worcestershire sauce, adding a splash of water if you think the mixture is too dry. Scrape everything into your slow cooker.

3 Spoon the mash on top of the mince mixture, cover and cook on low for 5 hrs – the mixture should be bubbling at the sides when it is ready. Crisp up the potato topping under the grill, if you like, then serve with green vegetables.

4 Once cooled, this will keep frozen in an airtight container for up to two months. Defrost thoroughly in the fridge and reheat until piping hot.

NUTRITIONAL INFO

PER SERVING KCAL **438** | FAT **10G** | SATURATES **4G** | CARBS **57G** | SUGARS **12G** | FIBRE **11G** | PROTEIN **23G** | SALT **0.39G**

Sticky Spiced Lamb Shanks

Prep: 15 mins
Cook: 9 hrs and 30 mins–10 hrs and 30 mins

Serves 2

1½ tbsp olive oil
2 lamb shanks
3 onions, sliced
4 garlic cloves, sliced
½ cinnamon stick
1 tbsp cumin seeds, crushed
1 tbsp coriander seeds, crushed
pinch of chilli flakes
400g (14oz) can chopped tomatoes
500ml (18fl oz) chicken or vegetable stock
2 tbsp pomegranate molasses
4 dried apricots, chopped
4 dried figs, chopped
handful of coriander, chopped
rice, to serve

1 Heat the oil in a large frying pan over a high heat and cook the shanks for 2–3 mins until browned all over. Place in your slow cooker with all the other ingredients except the coriander, cover and cook on low for 9–10 hrs until the meat is falling off the bones.

2 Remove the shanks from the slow cooker and wrap in foil to keep warm. Continue to cook down the juices, uncovered, until thick and saucy. Season, then serve the shanks scattered with the coriander alongside some rice.

NUTRITIONAL INFO
PER SERVING KCAL **1114** | FAT **55G** | SATURATES **23G** | CARBS **64G** | SUGARS **52G** | FIBRE **10G** | PROTEIN **95G** | SALT **1.93G**

Melt-in-the-Mouth Pork Belly

Prep: 20 mins
Cook: 4 hrs and 20 mins

Serves 6

1–1.2kg (2lb 4oz–2lb 10oz) pork belly joint
3 garlic cloves, crushed
thumb-sized piece of ginger, peeled and finely grated
3 tsp sea salt flakes
1 tbsp soy sauce
2 onions, sliced

To serve
mashed potato
seasonal vegetables
apple sauce
gravy (see Tip below)

TIP

To make a gravy, pour the remaining cooking juices from the slow cooker into a large jug and leave to settle for 2–3 mins. Pour off the layer of fat that will rise to the top, leaving the meat juices behind. Put the cooked onion slices from the slow cooker in a frying pan over a high heat for 3–4 mins until starting to caramelize, then add 1 tsp plain flour. Stir to coat the onions, then add the reserved meat juices and cook until the gravy becomes glossy and thick.

1. Cut the pork belly into 3 long strips, then remove the skin but leave the fat in place. Mix together the garlic, ginger, salt and soy sauce, then rub the mixture all over the pork belly. Put the sliced onions into the bottom of your slow cooker and place the pork belly pieces on top. Cover and cook on high for 4 hrs.
2. Carefully take the pork belly out of the slow cooker, then transfer to a nonstick frying pan with a good spoonful of the cooking juices. Leave to sizzle away on a high heat, turning occasionally, until all sides are browned and the liquid has evaporated.
3. Serve the meat with mashed potato, seasonal vegetables, apple sauce and some gravy.

NUTRITIONAL INFO

PER SERVING KCAL **540** | FAT **40G** | SATURATES **15G** | CARBS **4G** | SUGARS **3G** | FIBRE **1G** | PROTEIN **39G** | SALT **3.15G**

Pork Fillet with Apples

Prep: 15 mins
Cook: 4 hrs and 10 mins

Serves 4

½ tbsp rapeseed oil
500g (1lb 2oz) pork fillet, sliced into medallions
1 onion, finely chopped
150ml (5fl oz) low-salt chicken stock
1 tbsp Dijon mustard
3 eating apples, cored and quartered
4 sage leaves, finely sliced
2 tbsp half-fat crème fraiche
vegetables, to serve

1 Heat the oil in a large frying pan over a high heat, then fry the pork medallions for 2 mins on each side until they pick up a little colour. Add the onion and cook for a few minutes, then add the stock and mustard to the pan and stir. Tip the pork and sauce into your slow cooker.

2 Add the apples and sage and season with black pepper. Cover and cook on low for 4 hrs or until the meat is tender, then stir in the crème fraiche and serve with some simple vegetables.

NUTRITIONAL INFO

PER SERVING KCAL **344** | FAT **14G** | SATURATES **5G** | CARBS **18G** | SUGARS **13G** | FIBRE **5G** | PROTEIN **33G** | SALT **0.65G**

Budget-Friendly Coq Au Vin

Prep: 30 mins
Cook: 3 hrs and 30 mins–8 hrs and 30 mins

Serves 4

8 bone-in, skin-on chicken thighs
30g (1oz) butter
140g (5oz) smoked bacon or pancetta, chopped
400g (14oz) pearl onions or small shallots, peeled
2 large or 4 small carrots, cut into chunks
2 garlic cloves, crushed
3 tbsp plain flour
1 tbsp tomato purée
300ml (10fl oz) chicken stock
600ml (20fl oz) red wine
2 bay leaves
1 large thyme sprig
300g (10½oz) button mushrooms
handful of parsley leaves, chopped (optional)
mashed potato or buttered tagliatelle, to serve

1 Season the chicken. Melt half the butter in a deep frying pan over a medium heat and cook the chicken, skin side down, in batches if necessary, for 10 mins until deep golden. Flip to seal the fleshy side for a few minutes, then place in your slow cooker.

2 Tip the bacon into the same pan and fry for 5–6 mins until crisp, then add to the slow cooker. Tip the onions or shallots and carrots into the pan and fry in the bacon fat for 5 mins until starting to colour. Add the garlic and cook for 1 min more, then sprinkle over the flour and cook for 1–2 mins until you have a sandy paste. Stir through the tomato purée and cook for 2 mins more.

3 Pour the stock and wine into the pan and bring to the boil, then pour into the slow cooker. Nestle in the bay leaves and thyme and season, then cover and cook on high for 3–4 hrs or on low for 7–8 hrs, stirring once or twice, until the chicken is tender.

4 While the chicken cooks, heat the remaining butter in a clean frying pan and fry the mushrooms for 4–5 mins over a medium heat. Tip into the slow cooker about an hour before the end of cooking and stir. Scatter over the parsley, if using, and serve with mashed potato or buttered tagliatelle.

5 Once cooled, the coq au vin can be kept chilled in an airtight container for up to three days or frozen for up to three months. Defrost thoroughly in the fridge and reheat in a saucepan over a medium heat until piping hot.

NUTRITIONAL INFO

PER SERVING KCAL **678** | FAT **35G** | SATURATES **12G** | CARBS **21G** | SUGARS **9G** | FIBRE **6G** | PROTEIN **39G** | SALT **2.1G**

Saucy Chicken & Vegetables

Prep: 15 mins
Cook: 2 hrs and 30 mins

Serves 2

- 1 tbsp olive oil
- 2 skin-on chicken breasts
- 200g (7oz) new potatoes, thinly sliced
- 250ml (9fl oz) chicken stock
- 200g (7oz) mixed spring vegetables (broccoli, peas, broad beans and sliced courgette)
- 2 tbsp crème fraîche
- handful of tarragon leaves, roughly chopped

TIP

For a mustardy sauce, stir 1 tbsp wholegrain mustard in with the crème fraîche.

1. Heat the oil in a frying pan over a high heat, add the chicken, skin side down, and cook for 5 mins until golden. Turn the chicken over, then add the potatoes and stir to coat in the oil. Spread the potatoes in the bottom of your slow cooker, sit the chicken on top and pour over the stock, then cover and cook on high for 1 hr 30 mins.
2. Remove the chicken and stir the vegetables in with the potatoes. Put the chicken back on top and cook for another 1 hr until cooked through. Stir in the crème fraîche to make a creamy sauce, season with pepper and salt, if you like, and add the tarragon. Serve immediately.

NUTRITIONAL INFO

PER SERVING KCAL **386** | FAT **16G** | SATURATES **6G** | CARBS **23G** | SUGARS **0G** | FIBRE **3G** | PROTEIN **38G** | SALT **1.5G**

Honey & Mustard Chicken Thighs

Prep: 10 mins
Cook: 4 hrs and 20 mins

Serves 4–6

1 tbsp butter
8 bone-in, skin-on chicken thighs
8 spring onions, cut into lengths
150ml (5fl oz) chicken stock
1 tbsp Dijon mustard
2 tbsp honey
2 tbsp double cream or crème fraîche
100g (3½oz) frozen peas
crusty bread, to serve

1 Melt the butter in a frying pan and quickly brown the chicken thighs all over. Make sure the skin picks up plenty of colour. Season, then put them in your slow cooker. Brown the spring onions and add them to the slow cooker as well. Add the stock, mustard and honey, cover and cook on low for 4 hrs.

2 Stir in the cream or crème fraîche and peas, then cook for a further 15 mins with the lid off. Crisp up the chicken skin under the grill, if you like, then serve with crusty bread.

NUTRITIONAL INFO

PER SERVING (IF SERVING 4) KCAL **332** | FAT **16G** | SATURATES **8G** | CARBS **11G** | SUGARS **10G** | FIBRE **2G** | PROTEIN **35G** | SALT **0.9G**

Turkey Breasts with Wine & Bacon

Prep: 1 hr
Cook: 3 hrs and 15 mins–4 hrs and 15 mins

Serves 8

2 turkey breast fillets (800–900g/1lb 12oz–2lb each)
16 smoked streaky bacon rashers
2 tbsp thyme leaves, plus extra to serve
1 tbsp sunflower oil
1 onion, thickly sliced
2 carrots, sliced
2 bay leaves
15g (½oz) dried porcini mushrooms
150ml (5fl oz) dry white wine
500ml (18fl oz) chicken stock
2 tbsp plain flour

To serve
roast potatoes
seasonal vegetables
cranberry sauce

1 Lay a length of string twice the length of a turkey fillet on a chopping board. Arrange four more lengths of kitchen string large enough to tie around the width of the fillet at intervals across your first string, winding each one around the main string once so that they don't move around too much. Lay eight rashers of bacon across the main string and running in the same direction as the four shorter strings, overlapping the rashers slightly. Scatter with 1 tbsp thyme and grind over some black pepper.

2 Place a turkey fillet on top of the bacon, then wrap the bacon around it and tie the strings around the middle and around the length to hold everything in place – it should be snug but not too tight. Snip off any excess string with scissors.

3 Heat the oil in a large frying pan and fry the fillet on all sides until browned, then remove from the pan. Meanwhile, wrap and tie the other fillet, then brown that too. Set aside.

4 Add the onion and carrots to the pan and cook until starting to colour. Tip the vegetables into your slow cooker (we used one with a capacity of 3.5 litres/6 pints) and add the bay leaves and mushrooms, then arrange the turkey fillets on top. Pour the wine and stock into the frying pan and bring to a rapid boil. Pour into your slow cooker, cover and cook on low for 3–4 hrs until cooked through.

5 Lift the turkey fillets onto a plate and cover with foil. Mix the flour with 4 tbsp water to make a smooth liquid. Strain the cooking juices from the slow cooker into a saucepan, whisk in the flour mixture and keep whisking over the heat while bringing to a simmer to make a thin gravy. Serve with the sliced turkey fillets, roast potatoes, seasonal vegetables and cranberry sauce.

NUTRITIONAL INFO
PER SERVING KCAL **297** | FAT **12G** | SATURATES **4G** | CARBS **7G** | SUGARS **3G** | FIBRE **1G** | PROTEIN **35G** | SALT **1.9G**

Prawn, Pea & Tomato Curry

Prep: 15 mins
Cook: 3 hrs and 30 mins–4 hrs

Serves 4

1 tbsp vegetable oil
large thumb-sized piece of ginger, peeled and chopped
6 garlic cloves, roughly chopped
3 tbsp tikka masala curry paste
6 ripe tomatoes, each cut into 8 wedges
2 onions, each cut into 12 wedges
400g (14oz) peeled raw king prawns
250g (9oz) frozen peas
small bunch of coriander, chopped
rice, to serve

1 Place the oil in a mini blender with the ginger, garlic, curry paste and all but 8 tomato wedges and blitz to a paste. Scrape into your slow cooker and stir in the onions. Cover and cook on high for 3 hrs.

2 Stir in the remaining tomato wedges, the prawns and peas, then cover and cook on high for 30 mins–1 hr until the prawns are cooked through.

3 Scatter with the coriander, then serve with rice.

NUTRITIONAL INFO

PER SERVING KCAL **210** | FAT **6G** | SATURATES **0.5G** | CARBS **18G** | SUGARS **12G** | FIBRE **8G** | PROTEIN **17G** | SALT **1.53G**

V

Mushroom Risotto

Prep: 15 mins
Cook: 3 hrs and 20 mins

Serves 4

1 tsp olive oil
1 onion, finely chopped
250g (9oz) chestnut mushrooms, sliced
1 litre (1¾ pints) vegetable stock, plus extra if needed
50g (1¾oz) dried porcini mushrooms
300g (10½oz) wholegrain rice
small bunch of parsley, finely chopped
grated parmesan (or vegetarian alternative), to serve

1. Heat the oil in a frying pan and fry the onion with a splash of water for 10 mins or until soft but not coloured. Add the mushroom slices and stir them around until they start to soften and release their juices.
2. Meanwhile, pour the stock into a saucepan and add the porcini, bring to a simmer and then leave to soak. Tip the onion and mushrooms into your slow cooker and add the rice, then stir it in well. Pour over the stock and porcini, leaving any sediment in the saucepan.
3. Cover and cook on high for 3 hrs, stirring halfway through cooking, then check the consistency – the rice should be cooked. If it needs a little more liquid, stir in a splash more stock. Stir in the parsley and season. Serve with grated parmesan.

NUTRITIONAL INFO

PER SERVING KCAL **346** | FAT **3G** | SATURATES **0.3G** | CARBS **67G** | SUGARS **5G** | FIBRE **5G** | PROTEIN **10G** | SALT **0.53G**

V

Prep: 15 mins
Cook: 4 hrs and 20 mins–6 hrs and 20 mins

Creamy Potato Gratin

Serves 4–6

25g (1oz) butter
1 garlic clove, crushed
1kg (2lb 4oz) floury potatoes, such as Maris Piper, very thinly sliced
300ml (10fl oz) double cream
200ml (7fl oz) whole milk
50g (1¾oz) parmesan (or vegetarian alternative), grated
small handful of parsley, finely chopped

1 Melt the butter in a large pan over a medium–low heat and fry the garlic for 1 min until softened. Tip in the sliced potatoes, cream and milk and season well with salt and freshly ground black pepper. Stir continuously for 5–10 mins until the cream and milk are steaming and the liquid has thickened (it should coat the back of a spoon). Scatter in the cheese and stir until melted.

2 Tip into your slow cooker and push the potatoes down until submerged in the liquid. Cover and cook on high for 4 hrs or low for 6 hrs until tender. To brown, gently transfer to an ovenproof dish and grill on high for 5–10 mins. Serve scattered with the chopped parsley.

3 Once cooled, this will keep covered and chilled for two days. Cut into portions and reheat in an oven at 180°C/160°C fan/350°F/Gas Mark 4 for 20 mins until piping hot through. Brown under a hot grill for 5–10 mins.

NUTRITIONAL INFO
PER SERVING (IF SERVING 6) KCAL **481** | FAT **34G** | SATURATES **21G** | CARBS **34G** | SUGARS **4G** | FIBRE **3G** | PROTEIN **8G** | SALT **0.3G**

Soups & Stews

Pea & Ham Soup

*

Prep: 10 mins
Cook: 2 hrs and 30 mins–8 hrs and 30 mins

Serves 6–8

1 onion, chopped
250g (9oz) leeks, sliced
2 bay leaves
450g (1lb) cooked or raw ham joint
1.4 litres (2½ pints) hot low-salt vegetable stock or water
750g (1lb 10oz) frozen peas, defrosted

1 Tip the onion, leeks, bay leaves and ham into your slow cooker. Pour over the hot vegetable stock or water, cover and cook on high for 2 hrs or low for 6 hrs. If starting with raw ham, cook the soup for an additional 45 mins on high or 2 hrs on low.

2 Remove the ham and set aside. Pour the peas into the slow cooker, cover and cook on high for 30 mins more until the peas are cooked through. Meanwhile, shred the ham with your hands or two forks.

3 Remove the bay leaves from the soup and discard, then transfer the soup to a blender and blitz.

4 Once completely cool, the pea soup (without the ham) can be frozen for up to three months. Defrost thoroughly in the fridge overnight, then reheat in a saucepan until piping hot.

5 Season the soup to taste, then divide between bowls and scatter some of the shredded ham over each bowl before serving.

NUTRITIONAL INFO

PER SERVING (IF SERVING 8) KCAL **165** | FAT **3G** | SATURATES **1G** | CARBS **14G** | SUGARS **9G** | FIBRE **7G** | PROTEIN **17G** | SALT **1.6G**

Rustic Chicken Soup

Prep: 15 mins
Cook: 2 hrs and 45 mins– 3 hrs and 45 mins

Serves 4

1 tbsp olive oil
2 onions, chopped
3 carrots, chopped
1 tbsp thyme leaves, roughly chopped
1 litre (1¾ pints) chicken stock
1 roast chicken carcass, meat removed (optional)
300g (10½oz) leftover roast chicken, shredded and skin removed
200g (7oz) frozen peas
3 tbsp Greek yogurt
1 garlic clove, crushed
squeeze of lemon juice
cheese and spinach scone wedges, to serve

1 Heat the olive oil in a large frying pan over a low heat, add the onions, carrots and thyme and fry for 15 mins until softened. Tip them into your slow cooker with the stock and add the chicken carcass, if using. Season, cover and cook on high for 2–3 hrs until the vegetables are tender.

2 Remove and discard the carcass, if used, then stir the leftover roast chicken and frozen peas into the soup and cook for 30 mins more. Remove half the mixture and purée with a stick blender, then stir back into the soup. At this stage, once cooled, the soup will keep frozen in an airtight container for up to two months. Defrost thoroughly in the fridge and reheat gently in a saucepan until piping hot, then finish as below.

3 Mix the yogurt, garlic and lemon juice together and season. Ladle the soup into bowls, swirl in the garlic yogurt and serve with wedges of cheese and spinach scones.

NUTRITIONAL INFO

PER SERVING KCAL **339** | FAT **13G** | SATURATES **5G** | CARBS **18G** | SUGARS **11G** | FIBRE **7G** | PROTEIN **34G** | SALT **2.23G**

V

Prep: 15 mins
Cook: 3 hrs and 15 mins–5 hrs and 15 mins

Broccoli & Cheese Soup

Serves 6

- 1 tbsp vegetable or sunflower oil
- 1 onion, chopped
- 2 garlic cloves, crushed
- 250g (9oz) potatoes, roughly chopped
- 325g (11½oz) broccoli, roughly chopped
- 750ml (1⅓ pints) vegetable stock
- 150g (5½oz) mature cheddar, chopped
- 125ml (4fl oz) single cream, plus extra to serve
- griddled or crusty bread, to serve

TIP

Swap the cheddar for blue cheese if you prefer a punchier flavour.

1 Heat the oil in a frying pan over a medium–low heat and fry the onion for 10–12 mins until soft but not golden. Stir in the garlic and fry for 1 min, then stir in the potatoes and cook for a few minutes to soften slightly. Tip into your slow cooker.

2 Add the broccoli and stock to the slow cooker and season well with salt and black pepper. Cook on high for 3 hrs or on low for 5 hrs. The broccoli should be tender but the stalk may still have a bit of bite. Add the cheese and stir until melted, then stir through the cream.

3 Pour the soup into a blender and blend until smooth. Serve with a swirl of cream, a grinding of black pepper and griddled or crusty bread on the side for dunking.

NUTRITIONAL INFO

PER SERVING KCAL **236** | FAT **15G** | SATURATES **8G** | CARBS **11G** | SUGARS **3G** | FIBRE **3G** | PROTEIN **13G** | SALT **1.2G**

✻ V

Prep: 10 mins
Cook: 3 hrs

Spiced Carrot & Lentil Soup

Serves 4

2 tsp cumin seeds
pinch of chilli flakes
2 tbsp olive oil
600g (1lb 5oz) carrots, coarsely grated
140g (5oz) dried split red lentils, rinsed
700ml (1¼ pints) hot vegetable stock
125ml (4fl oz) milk

To serve

coriander leaves
natural yogurt
naan

TIP

Substitute the cumin seeds and chilli flakes for a few teaspoons of harissa paste to give a Moroccan flavour.

1. Place half the cumin seeds, half the chilli flakes, the oil, carrots, lentils and stock into your slow cooker. Cover and cook on high for 3 hrs until the lentils are tender.
2. Dry-fry the remaining cumin seeds and chilli flakes in a small frying pan just until fragrant.
3. When the lentils are done, stir in the milk. Transfer to a blender and blitz until smooth (or leave it chunky if you prefer).
4. Season to taste and serve with a dollop of natural yogurt, a sprinkling of the reserved toasted spices and warmed naans.
5. Once cooled, this soup will keep chilled in an airtight container for up to three days or frozen for up to three months. Defrost thoroughly in the fridge and stir well when reheating in a saucepan until piping hot, to bring it back together.

NUTRITIONAL INFO

PER SERVING KCAL **263** | FAT **8G** | SATURATES **2G** | CARBS **31G** | SUGARS **13G** | FIBRE **9G** | PROTEIN **11G** | SALT **0.91G**

✱ V Ve

Spiced Parsnip Soup

Prep: 15 mins
Cook: 8 hrs

Serves 6

750g (1lb 10oz) parsnips, peeled and chopped
400g (14oz) carrots, peeled and chopped
1 onion, chopped
2 large garlic cloves, crushed
1–2 tbsp curry powder, or to taste
1 litre (1¾ pints) vegetable stock

1 Tip the parsnips, carrots, onion, garlic and curry powder into your slow cooker and mix well so that all the vegetables are coated in the curry powder. Pour in the vegetable stock, then mix again and season well.

2 Cover and cook on low for 8 hrs. If you prefer your soup a little looser, stir in a few splashes of boiled water. Divide between bowls and season with black pepper before serving.

3 Once completely cool, the soup will keep chilled in an airtight container for three days or frozen for up to three months. Defrost thoroughly in the fridge, then reheat in a saucepan until piping hot before serving.

NUTRITIONAL INFO

PER SERVING KCAL **155** | FAT **2G** | SATURATES **0.3G** | CARBS **24G** | SUGARS **14G** | FIBRE **11G** | PROTEIN **4G** | SALT **0.5G**

✱ V

Leek & Potato Soup

Prep: 15 mins
Cook: 3 hrs and 15 mins–7 hrs and 15 mins

Serves 4

50g (1¾oz) butter
1 onion, finely sliced
2 leeks, halved and sliced, green tops reserved (see Tip below)
1 bay leaf
300–400g (10½–14oz) floury potatoes, such as Maris Piper, cut into small chunks
1.2 litres (2 pints) vegetable stock
2 tbsp crème fraîche

TIP

To make a crispy leek garnish, wash the dark green top from one of the leeks and dry thoroughly. Slice as thinly as you can, then scatter over a microwave-proof plate. Drizzle lightly with sunflower oil, season with a pinch of salt and microwave on full power for 3–4 mins, checking and tossing every minute or so, until crisp and golden. Leave to cool, then scatter over the soup.

1 Melt the butter in a frying pan over a medium heat. Cook the onion, leeks and bay leaf with a pinch each of salt and black pepper for 10–15 mins, stirring occasionally, until all the veg is soft. Transfer the softened veg and bay leaf to your slow cooker.

2 Add the potatoes and stock and stir, then cover and cook on high for 3–4 hrs or on low for 6–7 hrs until the potatoes are completely soft.

3 Remove the bay leaf from the soup, then add the crème fraîche. Transfer to a blender and blitz until smooth. Taste for seasoning and adjust as needed. Ladle the soup into bowls, then top with a grinding of black pepper to serve.

4 Once cooled, this soup will keep chilled in an airtight container for three days or frozen for up to three months. Defrost thoroughly in the fridge before reheating until piping hot.

NUTRITIONAL INFO

PER SERVING KCAL **250** | FAT **14G** | SATURATES **9G** | CARBS **23G** | SUGARS **7G** | FIBRE **6G** | PROTEIN **4G** | SALT **0.99G**

✱ V Ve

Prep: 15 mins
Cook: 8 hrs and 10 mins–15 hrs and 10 mins

Velvety Pumpkin Soup

Serves 6

- 2 tbsp rapeseed oil
- 3 onions, chopped
- 30g (1oz) ginger, peeled and chopped
- 3 large garlic cloves, chopped
- 1½–2 tbsp medium curry powder
- 1 tsp ground coriander
- ½ tsp crushed dried chillies (optional)
- 1kg (2lb 4oz) pumpkin or butternut squash, peeled, deseeded and cut into chunks
- 1 tbsp vegetable bouillon powder
- 400ml (14fl oz) coconut milk
- 180g (6¼oz) dried red lentils
- 15g (½oz) coriander, chopped
- crusty bread, to serve

1 Heat the oil in a large pan over a medium heat and fry the onions and ginger for 10 mins, stirring occasionally, until softened and starting to colour. Stir in the garlic, curry powder, ground coriander and dried chillies, if using, and cook for 1 min more.

2 Tip the mixture into a large slow cooker along with all the remaining ingredients, except the chopped coriander. Add 2 litres (3½ pints) water, cover and cook on high for 8 hrs or on low overnight for 15 hrs. Transfer to a blender and blitz until smooth. Ladle into bowls, scatter over the coriander and serve with crusty bread.

3 Once completely cool, the soup will keep chilled in an airtight container for two days or frozen for up to two months. Defrost thoroughly in the fridge before reheating in a saucepan over a low heat or in the microwave until piping hot.

TIP

If your pumpkin or squash isn't quite big enough to make up the required weight, you can supplement it with chopped carrots.

NUTRITIONAL INFO

PER SERVING KCAL **260** | FAT **10G** | SATURATES **5G** | CARBS **29G** | SUGARS **8G** | FIBRE **7G** | PROTEIN **10G** | SALT **0.7G**

Beef Stew with Dumplings

Prep: 20 mins
Cook: 5 hrs and 20 mins–8 hrs and 20 mins

Serves 4

2 tbsp vegetable oil
800g (1lb 12oz) stewing beef, roughly chopped
2 onions, roughly chopped
4 carrots, roughly chopped
2 celery sticks, roughly chopped
150ml (5fl oz) red wine
a few sprigs of rosemary and thyme
2 bay leaves
½ tsp Worcestershire sauce
850ml (1½ pints) beef stock
small handful of parsley, chopped
wilted chard, to serve

For the dumplings
150g (5½oz) self-raising flour
70g (2½oz) shredded suet

1 Heat 1 tbsp oil in a large frying pan over a medium heat and brown the beef all over – you may need to do this in batches. Transfer to your slow cooker, leaving any oil behind. Add the remaining oil to the pan, turn the heat to medium–low and fry the onions, carrots and celery for 10–12 mins until softened but not golden. Add to the slow cooker.

2 Pour the wine into the pan and bring to a simmer. Cook for 2 mins before pouring into the slow cooker. Add the remaining stew ingredients to the slow cooker, cover and cook on high for 4 hrs or on low for 7 hrs.

3 Shortly before the cooking time is up, make the dumplings. Put the flour and suet in a bowl and season well with salt and black pepper. Mix to combine, then make a well in the centre and pour in 3 tbsp cold water. Stir, then gradually add a teaspoon of water at a time until the mix easily comes together into a soft dough. Form into 8 balls and carefully put on top of the stew. Cook for a further 1 hr, then scatter with the parsley and serve with wilted chard.

4 Once cooled, the stew and dumplings will keep frozen in two separate airtight containers for up to two months. Defrost thoroughly in the fridge. Reheat the stew first until piping hot, then arrange the dumplings on top and continue cooking until they are piping hot too.

NUTRITIONAL INFO

PER SERVING KCAL **707** | FAT **35G** | SATURATES **14G** | CARBS **41G** | SUGARS **9G** | FIBRE **7G** | PROTEIN **46G** | SALT **0.8G**

Campfire Stew

Prep: 15 mins, plus soaking
Cook: 6 hrs and 25 mins–8 hrs and 25 mins

Serves 6

600g (1lb 5oz) gammon joint
1 tbsp vegetable oil
2 onions, roughly chopped
2 carrots, chopped
1 celery stick, chopped
1 red pepper, chopped
1 yellow pepper, chopped
3 garlic cloves, crushed
1 tbsp tomato purée
2 tsp smoked paprika
½ tsp chilli powder (optional)
2 × 400g (14oz) cans chopped tomatoes
1 tbsp Worcestershire sauce
1 tbsp golden caster sugar
2 bay leaves
2 × 400g (14oz) cans haricot beans, drained and rinsed
baked potatoes topped with butter, to serve

1 Remove the skin and fat from the gammon, then soak in a pan of water in the fridge overnight – this will remove some of the salt.

2 Heat the oil in a large frying pan over a medium–high heat and cook the onions, carrots and celery for 10 mins, stirring regularly, until the veg start to soften. Stir in the peppers, garlic, tomato purée, paprika and chilli powder, if using. Cook for another 2 mins, then add the tomatoes and stir. Season well and stir in the Worcestershire sauce, sugar and bay leaves.

3 Transfer the stew to your slow cooker, cover and cook on low for 6–8 hrs. Turn the heat to high and add the beans, then cook for a further 10 mins. Shred the gammon using two forks, stir into the beans and serve immediately with baked potatoes topped with butter.

4 To store, leave to cool completely and chill in an airtight container for up to three days or freeze for up to two months. Defrost thoroughly in the fridge before reheating until piping hot.

NUTRITIONAL INFO

PER SERVING KCAL **327** | FAT **12G** | SATURATES **3G** | CARBS **25G** | SUGARS **15G** | FIBRE **11G** | PROTEIN **25G** | SALT **2.28G**

Chicken, Bacon & Potato Stew

Prep: 20 mins
Cook: 4 hrs and 30 mins–6 hrs and 30 mins

Serves 6

1 tbsp olive oil
6 bone-in, skinless chicken thighs
12 smoked streaky bacon rashers, chopped
200g (7oz) shallots, peeled
350g (12oz) baby new potatoes, halved if large
a few thyme sprigs
200ml (7fl oz) white wine
500ml (18fl oz) hot chicken stock
2 tbsp chopped tarragon
280ml (9½fl oz) buttermilk (optional)
squeeze of lemon juice

1 Heat the oil in a large frying pan over a medium heat and brown the chicken thighs for about 10 mins until they have a nice golden colour, then remove and set aside. Add the bacon and shallots to the pan and brown these too.

2 Tip into your slow cooker with the chicken, potatoes, thyme, wine, stock and 1 tbsp tarragon and season well. Cover and cook on high for 4–6 hrs until the chicken is tender and falling off the bone.

3 Check the sauce: if you like it a little thicker, strain the liquid into a pan and boil until thickened, then return to the slow cooker. Add the buttermilk, if using, and whisk until smooth. Sprinkle in the lemon juice and remaining tarragon and check the seasoning before serving.

NUTRITIONAL INFO

PER SERVING KCAL **284** | FAT **13G** | SATURATES **4G** | CARBS **12G** | SUGARS **4G** | FIBRE **2G** | PROTEIN **2G** | SALT **1.7G**

✱

Prep: 20 mins
Cook: 2 hrs

Mexican-Style Chicken Stew

Serves 4

1 tbsp vegetable oil
1 onion, finely chopped
3 garlic cloves, finely chopped
½ tsp dark brown soft sugar
1 tsp chipotle paste
400g (14oz) can chopped tomatoes
4 skinless chicken breasts
1 small red onion, sliced into rings
a few coriander leaves
corn tortillas or rice, to serve

1 Heat the oil in a frying pan over a low heat and cook the finely chopped onion for 5 mins or until softened and starting to turn golden, adding the garlic for the final minute. Transfer to your slow cooker with the sugar, chipotle paste, tomatoes and chicken. Cover and cook on high for 2 hrs.

2 Remove the chicken and shred with two forks, then stir back into the sauce. At this stage, once cooled, the stew will keep frozen in an airtight container for up to two months. Defrost thoroughly in the fridge and reheat until piping hot before finishing as below.

3 Scatter with a little red onion and the coriander and serve with the remaining red onion and some corn tortillas or rice.

NUTRITIONAL INFO

PER SERVING KCAL **203** | FAT **5G** | SATURATES **1G** | CARBS **6G** | SUGARS **4G** | FIBRE **2G** | PROTEIN **35G** | SALT **0.37G**

✻ V

Prep: 20 mins
Cook: 5hrs and 15 mins–
6 hrs and 15 mins

Vegetable Stew with Cheddar Dumplings

Serves 6

2 tbsp olive oil
200g (7oz) baby carrots, halved if large
3 leeks, thickly sliced
3 garlic cloves, crushed
3 tbsp plain flour
400ml (14fl oz) vegetable stock
2 courgettes, cut into large chunks
2 × 400g (14oz) cans butter or cannellini beans, drained and rinsed
1 bay leaf
4 thyme, rosemary or tarragon sprigs
200ml (7fl oz) crème fraîche
1 tbsp wholegrain mustard
200g (7oz) broad beans or peas
200g (7oz) spinach
½ small bunch of parsley, finely chopped

For the dumplings

100g (3½oz) self-raising flour
50g (1¾oz) vegetarian suet or cold butter, grated
100g (3½oz) mature cheddar, grated
½ small bunch of parsley, finely chopped

1 Heat 1 tbsp oil in a frying pan and fry the carrots for 5 mins until just golden, then tip into your slow cooker.

2 Heat the remaining oil in the pan and fry the leeks with a pinch of salt for 5 mins until soft. Add the garlic and stir in the flour. Gradually add the stock, stirring, until the flour has dissolved and there are no lumps. Bring to the boil, then tip into the slow cooker. Add the courgettes, beans and herbs and top up with water to cover the veg, if needed. Cover and cook on low for 4 hrs.

3 To make the dumplings, tip the flour into a bowl and stir in the suet or butter until evenly distributed. Add the cheese, parsley, ½ tsp cracked black pepper and a pinch of salt. Mix in 3–4 tbsp cold water with your hands to make a soft, slightly sticky dough (add a little more water if needed). Divide into six and roll into balls.

4 Add the crème fraîche, mustard, broad beans or peas and spinach to the slow cooker and turn it to high. Arrange the dumplings over the stew, cover and cook for 1–2 hrs until firm and doubled in size. Scatter with parsley and serve.

5 This will keep in an airtight container for up to three days in the fridge or in the freezer for up to three months. Freeze the stew and the dumplings separately. Defrost thoroughly in the fridge before reheating in the slow cooker until piping hot.

NUTRITIONAL INFO

PER SERVING KCAL **554** | FAT **33G** | SATURATES **17G** | CARBS **40G** | SUGARS **6G** | FIBRE **13G** | PROTEIN **18G** | SALT **0.9G**

Spanish-Style Chicken

Prep: 15 mins
Cook: 6 hrs and 20 mins

Serves 6

2 tbsp olive oil
1 Spanish onion, sliced
12 large bone-in, skinless chicken thighs
225g (8oz) chorizo picante, thickly sliced
3 mixed peppers, cut into chunks
150g (5½oz) Spanish pimiento-stuffed green olives
300ml (10fl oz) dry white wine
300ml (10fl oz) chicken stock
1 tbsp tomato purée
rice, to serve

1 Heat the olive oil in a large frying pan over a medium heat, add the onion and cook for about 5 mins until golden. Tip into your slow cooker (we used a 6.5 litre/11½ pint model), then fry the chicken thighs and chorizo picante in the same pan until starting to colour – you will need to do this in two batches.

2 Add to the slow cooker with the remaining ingredients. Scrape up any bits stuck to the bottom of the pan and tip into the slow cooker, then season, cover and cook on low for 6 hrs. Serve with rice.

NUTRITIONAL INFO
PER SERVING KCAL **447** | FAT **27G** | SATURATES **8G** | CARBS **7G** | SUGARS **6G** | FIBRE **4G** | PROTEIN **34G** | SALT **2.9G**

V Ve

Prep: 15 mins, plus soaking (optional)
Cook: 8 hrs and 15 mins–10 hrs and 25 mins

Aubergine & Chickpea Stew

Serves 4–6

- 200g (7oz) dried chickpeas or 2 × 400g (14oz) cans, drained and rinsed
- 2 tbsp extra virgin olive oil, plus extra to serve
- 2 onions, finely sliced
- 6 garlic cloves, crushed
- 1 tbsp baharat spice mix
- 1 tsp ground cinnamon
- small bunch of flat leaf parsley, leaves picked, stalks chopped
- 3 aubergines, cut into 2cm (¾ inch) rounds
- 2 × 400g (14oz) cans chopped tomatoes
- juice of 1 lemon
- 50g (1¾oz) toasted pine nuts
- pitta breads or flatbreads, to serve (optional)

1 If using dried chickpeas, soak them in cold water for 6–8 hrs. Drain the chickpeas and bring to the boil in a pan of salted water. Cook for 10 mins, then drain.

2 Heat the oil in a frying pan over a medium heat and fry the onions for 10 mins or until beginning to soften. Stir in the garlic, spice mix and cinnamon and cook for 1 min. Tip into your slow cooker and add the chickpeas, parsley stalks and aubergines. Add the tomatoes, then fill the tomato can with water, add to the pot and season. Cover and cook on high for 2 hrs, then turn the heat to low and cook for 6–8 hrs until the mixture has reduced slightly and the chickpeas and aubergines are really tender.

3 Stir in the lemon juice, then scatter over the pine nuts and parsley leaves. Drizzle over some extra olive oil and serve with pitta breads or flatbreads, if you like.

NUTRITIONAL INFO

PER SERVING (IF SERVING 6) KCAL **266** | FAT **10G** | SATURATES **1G** | CARBS **27G** | SUGARS **12G** | FIBRE **12G** | PROTEIN **11G** | SALT **0.1G**

Rich Paprika Seafood Bowl

Prep: 10 mins
Cook: 8 hrs and 30 mins–11 hrs

Serves 4

large bunch of flat leaf parsley, leaves and stalks separated

1 tbsp olive oil

2 onions, thinly sliced

2 celery sticks, finely chopped

2–3 tsp paprika

200g (7oz) roasted red peppers from a jar, thickly sliced

400g (14oz) can chopped tomatoes with garlic

a few fresh mussels (optional)

400g (14oz) skinless white fish fillets, cut into very large chunks

crusty bread, to serve

1 Whizz the parsley stalks, half the parsley leaves, the oil and seasoning together in a food processor. Place in your slow cooker with the onions, celery, paprika, peppers and tomatoes, cover and cook on low for 8–10 hrs. Nestle the mussels, if using, in the sauce and scatter the fish on top. Cover and cook on high for 30 mins–1 hr.

2 Discard any unopened mussels, then stir the fish into the sauce and serve immediately with some crusty bread.

NUTRITIONAL INFO

PER SERVING KCAL **200** | FAT **7G** | SATURATES **1G** | CARBS **11G** | SUGARS **8G** | FIBRE **5G** | PROTEIN **21G** | SALT **0.3G**

V Ve

Prep: 20 mins
Cook: 5 hrs and 20 mins–7 hrs and 20 mins

Healthy Chickpea Stew

Serves 4–6

1 tbsp vegetable or sunflower oil
1 red onion, sliced
2 garlic cloves, crushed
1 butternut squash (about 600g/1lb 5oz), peeled, deseeded and cut into chunks
½ tsp ground ginger
1 tsp ground cumin
1 tsp smoked paprika
1 tsp ground coriander
1 tsp ground turmeric
½ tsp ground cinnamon
400g (14oz) can chickpeas
400g (14oz) can chopped tomatoes
2 tbsp tomato purée
500ml (18fl oz) vegetable stock
handful of chopped coriander
couscous, to serve

1 Heat the oil in a large frying pan over a medium–low heat and fry the onion for 10–12 mins until softened and beginning to turn golden. Stir in the garlic and cook for 1 min, then add the squash and cook for a few minutes more to soften slightly. Scatter in the spices, stir to combine and cook for 2 mins until fragrant.

2 Tip everything into your slow cooker along with the chickpeas and their liquid, the tomatoes, tomato purée and the stock. Mix well, then cover and cook on high for 5 hrs or on low for 7 hrs.

3 Sprinkle with the chopped coriander and serve with couscous.

NUTRITIONAL INFO

PER SERVING (IF SERVING 6) KCAL **152** | FAT **4G** | SATURATES **0.3G** | CARBS **21G** | SUGARS **10G** | FIBRE **7G** | PROTEIN **6G** | SALT **0.3G**

Crowd Pleasers

Tender Beef Joint

Prep: 10 mins
Cook: 4 hrs and 40 mins–6 hrs and 45 mins

Serves 6–8

2 tsp vegetable oil
1kg (2lb 4oz) beef topside joint
125ml (4fl oz) white wine
2 carrots, roughly chopped
2 onions, quartered
2 rosemary sprigs
3 bay leaves
3 garlic cloves, peeled
500ml (18fl oz) beef stock
2 tbsp cornflour
1 tbsp tomato purée
seasonal vegetables, to serve

1 Heat the oil in a frying pan over a medium heat, then fry the beef on all sides until browned. Transfer the beef to a plate, then add the wine to the pan and scrape the sticky bits off the bottom. Set aside.

2 Put the carrots, onions, rosemary, bay leaves and garlic cloves in the bottom of your slow cooker and sit the beef on top. Pour in the wine and stock, then add a good pinch of salt and a few cracks of black pepper. Cover and cook on high for 4 hrs or on low for 6 hrs until the beef is cooked and tender. Remove from the slow cooker, cover and leave to rest for 30 mins.

3 Meanwhile, make the gravy. Strain the cooking juices through a colander over a large bowl or jug, then pour back into the slow cooker. Put the cornflour in a small bowl and stir in 2 tbsp of the juices to form a paste. Tip back into the slow cooker and whisk to ensure there are no lumps. Stir in the tomato purée and cook on high for 25–30 mins until thickened. Serve the gravy with the beef, along with some seasonal vegetables.

NUTRITIONAL INFO

PER SERVING (IF SERVING 8) KCAL **255** | FAT **11G** | SATURATES **4G** | CARBS **8G** | SUGARS **4G** | FIBRE **2G** | PROTEIN **27G** | SALT **0.3G**

Cinnamon & Orange Brisket

Prep: 20 mins
Cook: 6 hrs and 20 mins–7 hrs and 20 mins

Serves 6–8

zest and juice of 2 large oranges
2 large cinnamon sticks
2 large onions, thinly sliced
7 garlic cloves, peeled
1.5kg (3lb 5oz) beef brisket or blade steak
2 tsp ground cumin
1 tsp ground cinnamon
pinch of saffron threads
3 bay leaves
500ml (18fl oz) hot beef stock
3 tbsp soy sauce
2 tbsp red wine vinegar
2 tbsp honey
75g (2¾oz) light brown soft sugar
200g (7oz) fresh or frozen cranberries
handful of parsley, finely chopped
baked potatoes, rice or couscous, to serve

1 Put the squeezed orange halves into your slow cooker and add the cinnamon sticks, onions and garlic to cover the base. Season the beef all over, rub in the cumin and ground cinnamon and put in the slow cooker. Scatter over the saffron and bay leaves, then pour over the hot stock, soy sauce, vinegar, honey and orange zest and juice. Cover with the lid and cook on high for 4 hrs.

2 Remove the lid and stir in the sugar and cranberries. Cover and cook for a further 2–3 hrs on high until the beef is tender. Transfer the beef to a plate, then shred the meat with two forks, removing any fatty bits.

3 Pour the liquid into a wide pan and place over a high heat. Simmer for 15–20 mins until reduced by one-third, then season to taste. Remove the cinnamon sticks and bay leaves and discard. The oranges should have broken down into little pieces, but you can remove them if you prefer. Pour the sauce over the beef and toss together. At this stage, once cooled, the beef and sauce will keep frozen in an airtight container together for up to two months. Defrost thoroughly in the fridge and reheat gently until piping hot, adding a splash of water if needed.

4 Serve on a platter sprinkled with the chopped parsley, with baked potatoes, rice or couscous on the side.

NUTRITIONAL INFO

PER SERVING (IF SERVING 8) KCAL **411** | FAT **20G** | SATURATES **8G** | CARBS **22G** | SUGARS **20G** | FIBRE **3G** | PROTEIN **34G** | SALT **1G**

Gochujang Short Ribs with Apple Slaw

Prep: 30 mins
Cook: 4 hrs and 50 mins

Serves 4–6

1 tbsp vegetable oil
4 large beef short ribs (about 2kg/4lb 8oz)
2 garlic cloves
5 tbsp gochujang
3 tbsp dark soy sauce
3 tbsp dark brown soft sugar
1 cinnamon stick
2 star anise
1 tsp coriander seeds
5 tablespoons Shaohsing rice wine
2 red onions, quartered
thumb-sized piece of ginger, peeled and roughly chopped
400ml (14fl oz) beef stock
1 tbsp cornflour
2 spring onions, finely sliced
rice, to serve

For the slaw

2 apples, cored and cut into thin matchsticks
juice of 1 lemon

1 Heat the oil in a medium frying pan over a high heat. Season the short ribs all over with salt, then cook in the pan, in batches if necessary, for 8–10 mins until deep brown on all sides. Add a small splash of water to the pan in between batches, scrape up any bits stuck to the pan and pour the residual liquid into a small bowl. Set aside.

2 Lightly bash the garlic cloves with the skin still on. Mix the garlic with the gochujang, soy sauce, sugar, cinnamon, star anise, coriander seeds and rice wine. Tip into your slow cooker along with the red onions and ginger. Add the ribs, then pour over the stock. Cover and cook on low for 4 hrs 30 mins or until the meat is falling off the bone.

3 Towards the end of the cooking time, mix 1 tbsp of the reserved cooking liquid with the cornflour to make a smooth paste. Add this to the slow cooker when there is just 10 mins of cooking time remaining and mix well. Taste the sauce for seasoning and add more soy sauce, if needed. Cover and cook for the remaining time.

4 Meanwhile, make the slaw by mixing the apples with the lemon juice and season to taste.

5 Scoop the garlic cloves out of the slow cooker, discard the skins and stir the garlic back in. Serve the ribs with the spring onions sprinkled over, alongside rice and the slaw.

NUTRITIONAL INFO

PER SERVING (IF SERVING 6) KCAL **803** | FAT **62G** | SATURATES **25G** | CARBS **26G** | SUGARS **19G** | FIBRE **3G** | PROTEIN **34G** | SALT **1.9G**

Low & Slow Lamb Shoulder

Prep: 15 mins
Cook: 6 hrs and 45 mins–8 hrs and 45 mins

Serves 4–6

1.75kg (3lb 14oz) bone-in lamb shoulder
2 tsp vegetable or sunflower oil
200ml (7fl oz) red wine
2 carrots, roughly chopped
2 onions, quartered
2 celery sticks, roughly chopped
2 bay leaves
a few rosemary sprigs
a few thyme sprigs
300ml (10fl oz) lamb, chicken or vegetable stock
2 tbsp cornflour

To serve
roast potatoes
seasonal greens

1 Dry the lamb with a clean tea towel or kitchen paper, rub all over with the oil and season well with salt and black pepper. Heat a large frying pan over a medium heat and brown the lamb all over – this will take around 10–12 mins. Remove from the pan and set aside. Pour the wine into the pan and cook for 1–2 mins to cook off the alcohol.

2 Tip the veg and herbs into your slow cooker, then lay the lamb on top. Pour in the stock and wine. Cover and cook on high for 6 hrs or on low for 8 hrs, turning halfway through cooking if you can. Remove the lamb from the slow cooker, cover and leave to rest for 30 mins.

3 Meanwhile, make the gravy. Strain the cooking juices through a colander over a large bowl or jug, then pour back into the slow cooker (either discard the vegetables or eat them with the meal – they'll be soft but taste great). Put the cornflour in a small bowl and stir in 2 tbsp of the juices to form a paste. Tip back into the slow cooker and whisk to ensure there are no lumps. Cook on high for 25–30 mins until thickened. Serve the gravy with the lamb, roast potatoes and seasonal greens.

NUTRITIONAL INFO

PER SERVING (IF SERVING 6) KCAL **496** | FAT **33G** | SATURATES **15G** | CARBS **6G** | SUGARS **4G** | FIBRE **2G** | PROTEIN **36G** | SALT **0.3G**

Succulent Leg Of Lamb

Prep: 15 mins
Cook: 8 hrs and 15 mins

Serves 6

2 tbsp olive oil
1.3kg (3lb) boneless leg of lamb, tied
30g (1oz) unsalted butter
2 tbsp plain flour
300ml (10fl oz) lamb stock
200ml (7fl oz) red wine
2 red onions, cut into wedges
2 garlic cloves, sliced
5 thyme sprigs
5 rosemary sprigs

To serve
mashed potato
steamed green vegetables
mustard

1 Heat the oil in a large nonstick frying pan over a high heat, add the lamb and brown on all sides – this will take 4–6 mins. Melt the butter in a saucepan until foaming, then stir in the flour. Whisk in the stock gradually until incorporated, add the wine and bring to the boil. Set aside.

2 Put the onions, garlic, thyme and rosemary into your slow cooker and sit the lamb on top. Pour over the lamb gravy. Cover and cook on low for 8 hrs or until soft and tender.

3 Remove the lamb and set aside, covered, on a plate. Strain the liquid into a saucepan and simmer until slightly thickened. Thickly slice or shred the lamb with two forks and serve with the gravy, mashed potato and steamed green vegetables, with mustard on the side.

NUTRITIONAL INFO

PER SERVING KCAL **574** | FAT **37G** | SATURATES **16G** | CARBS **9G** | SUGARS **3G** | FIBRE **1G** | PROTEIN **43G** | SALT **0.3G**

*

Prep: 10 mins
Cook: 7–9 hrs

Moroccan Lamb Stew

Serves 6

- 2 tbsp olive or rapeseed oil
- 1kg (2lb 4oz) boneless lamb shoulder, cut into chunks
- 2 onions, sliced
- 5 garlic cloves, crushed
- thumb-sized piece of ginger, peeled and grated or finely chopped
- 1 tbsp ground cumin
- 1 tbsp ground coriander
- 1 tsp ground cinnamon
- pinch of saffron threads or turmeric
- ½ large or 1 small preserved lemon, flesh and pith scooped out and discarded, finely chopped
- 1 tbsp tomato purée
- 600ml (20fl oz) beef or lamb stock
- 1 tbsp honey
- zest of 1 lemon, plus a squeeze of juice
- 80g (2¾oz) pitted Kalamata olives
- handful of chopped mint, coriander or parsley (or a combination)
- couscous or rice, to serve

1. Heat 1 tbsp oil in a pan and brown the lamb in batches, transferring to the slow cooker as you go. Add the remaining oil and the onions to the pan and cook for 8–10 mins until softened.
2. Tip in the garlic and ginger and stir for 1–2 mins, then add the spices, preserved lemon and tomato purée. Warm through, then tip into the slow cooker. Swirl some water around the pan, then pour into the slow cooker along with the stock. Season, cover and cook on low for 6–8 hrs.
3. Once the meat is really tender, turn the heat up to high. Add the honey, lemon zest and juice and olives, cover and cook for 20–30 mins. At this stage, once cooled, the stew will keep frozen in an airtight container for up to two months. Defrost thoroughly in the fridge and reheat until piping hot.
4. Top with the herbs and serve with couscous or rice.

NUTRITIONAL INFO

PER SERVING KCAL **488** | FAT **35G** | SATURATES **14G** | CARBS **7G** | SUGARS **5G** | FIBRE **3G** | PROTEIN **34G** | SALT **1G**

✻

Prep: 25 mins, plus soaking
Cook: 6 hrs and 40 mins–8 hrs and 40 mins

Goat Mole Chilli with Pickled Radishes

Serves 6–8

2 dried ancho chillies
2 tbsp sunflower oil
1kg (2lb 4oz) boneless goat, cut into chunks
1 onion, finely chopped
3 garlic cloves, finely chopped
5 tomatoes, roughly chopped
2 cinnamon sticks
5 cloves
2 tsp ground cumin
1 tsp ground coriander
1 tsp dried oregano
1 tbsp chipotle paste
2 bay leaves
2 tbsp tomato purée
300ml (10fl oz) chicken stock
2 tbsp smooth peanut butter
30g (1oz) dark chocolate (70% cocoa solids), roughly chopped

For the radishes

2 tbsp apple cider vinegar
2 tbsp golden caster sugar
200g (7oz) radishes, finely sliced

1. Soak the ancho chillies in 100ml (3½fl oz) boiling water for 30 mins. Once softened, drain and chop, discarding the stems. Heat the oil in a large frying pan and add the goat. Cook in batches for 8–10 mins until browned all over, then transfer to your slow cooker using a slotted spoon.
2. Add the onion and garlic to the pan and cook for 8–10 mins until softened. Stir in the tomatoes, spices, oregano, chipotle paste, bay leaves, tomato purée, chicken stock, ½ tsp salt and the chopped ancho chillies and bring to the boil. Transfer to the slow cooker, cover and cook on high for 6–8 hrs until the goat is very tender and falls apart when stirred.
3. Meanwhile, for the radishes, mix the vinegar and sugar in a bowl with a pinch of salt until dissolved. Stir in the sliced radishes and some black pepper and leave to pickle for 15–20 mins.
4. Mix the peanut butter and dark chocolate into the mole and simmer for a further few minutes. At this stage, once cooled, the mole will keep frozen in an airtight container for up to two months. Defrost thoroughly in the fridge and reheat until piping hot before finishing as below.
5. Season the mole to taste and serve with the drained pickled radishes scattered over the top.

NUTRITIONAL INFO

PER SERVING (IF SERVING 8) KCAL **259** | FAT **10G** | SATURATES **3G** | CARBS **12G** | SUGARS **10G** | FIBRE **2G** | PROTEIN **29G** | SALT **0.9G**

Spiced Duck & Date Tagine

Prep: 15 mins
Cook: 5 hrs and 20 mins–7 hrs and 20 mins

Serves 6

2 tsp sunflower oil
6 skinless duck legs
1 large onion, peeled
2 garlic cloves, peeled
1 red chilli, deseeded
thumb-sized piece of ginger, peeled
1 tbsp ground cumin
1 tbsp ground coriander
1 tbsp ground cinnamon
1 tsp ground ginger
2 preserved lemons, flesh and pith scooped out and discarded
200g (7oz) pitted dates
400ml (14fl oz) passata
100g (3½oz) blanched almonds, very roughly chopped
a few mint leaves
couscous, to serve

1 Heat the oil in a frying pan and brown the duck legs in batches until golden, then transfer to your slow cooker. Meanwhile, put the onion, garlic, chilli, ginger, spices and preserved lemons in a food processor and blitz to a chunky paste. Tip the paste into the hot pan and cook for 5 mins to soften.

2 Add half the dates to the processor with 200ml (7fl oz) water and blitz until smooth. Cut the remaining dates into chunky pieces. Tip the onion paste and all the dates into the slow cooker, add the passata, season and stir. Cover and cook on low for 5–7 hrs.

3 Stir most of the almonds into the tagine, then serve with couscous, scattered with mint leaves and the remaining almonds.

NUTRITIONAL INFO

PER SERVING KCAL **527** | FAT **20G** | SATURATES **3G** | CARBS **30G** | SUGARS **27G** | FIBRE **5G** | PROTEIN **53G** | SALT **0.5G**

Honey & Mustard Pork

Prep: 30 mins, plus chilling
Cook: 5 hrs and 15 mins–6 hrs and 15 mins

Serves 4–6

1½ tsp fennel seeds
leaves from 3 thyme sprigs
2 garlic cloves, peeled
2 tbsp rapeseed or olive oil
1.8kg (4lb) pork loin, skin removed and fat well scored
300g (10½oz) shallots
1 small celeriac, peeled and cut into chunks
2 eating apples, such as Braeburn or Cox, peeled, cored and cut into wedges
150ml (5fl oz) white wine
250ml (9fl oz) chicken or pork stock
1 tbsp honey
1 tbsp Dijon mustard

To serve
roast potatoes
seasonal greens

1 Lightly crush the fennel seeds with the thyme leaves and the garlic using a pestle and mortar. Add 1 tbsp oil and plenty of salt and pepper, then bash to a rough paste. Rub all over the pork, then cover and chill for 2 hrs, or up to 24 hrs if you have time.

2 Pour a kettleful of boiling water over the shallots, then drain and set aside for 2 mins until cool enough to handle – this will make them easier to peel. Cut off the roots and remove the papery skins. Heat the remaining oil in a large frying pan and brown the shallots for a few minutes, then tip into your slow cooker. Add the celeriac and apples, season well and give them a mix.

3 Brown the pork in the same pan, on all sides, not forgetting the ends. Sit on top of the veg and apples, fat side up, nestling the joint in a little so that you can fit the lid on. Pour the wine into the frying pan and bubble for a minute, scraping the bottom of the pan to pick up any tasty bits. Pour in the stock, honey and mustard and bubble for another minute, then pour over the pork. Cover and cook on high for 3–4 hrs or on low for 5–6 hrs, turning the pork and stirring the veg halfway through cooking.

4 Remove the pork, wrap in foil and leave to rest for 10 mins before carving. Serve alongside the veg, with roast potatoes and seasonal greens.

NUTRITIONAL INFO

PER SERVING (IF SERVING 6) KCAL **597** | FAT **41G** | SATURATES **13G** | CARBS **9G** | SUGARS **9G** | FIBRE **4G** | PROTEIN **42G** | SALT **0.7G**

Goan Pulled Pork

Prep: 15 mins
Cook: 7 hrs and 10 mins–8 hrs and 10 mins

Serves 6

2 tbsp olive oil
1 large onion, sliced
1 garlic bulb, cloves peeled
thumb-sized piece of ginger, peeled and cut into very thin matchsticks
1 tbsp ground cumin
2 tbsp smoked paprika
2 tbsp ground coriander
½–1 tsp cayenne pepper (depending on how hot you like it)
225ml (8fl oz) apple cider vinegar
2kg (4lb 8oz) boneless pork leg or shoulder joint

For the salad

3 carrots, shredded or coarsely grated
1 red onion, finely chopped
3 tomatoes, chopped
generous handful of coriander
juice of 1 lemon
1 tbsp olive oil

To serve

12 chapatis or small wraps, warmed
cucumber raita
mango chutney

1 Heat the oil in a large frying pan over a medium–low heat. Fry the onion, garlic cloves and ginger for about 10 mins. Stir in the spices, pour in the vinegar and stir well. Tip into your slow cooker (we used a 6.5 litre/11½ pint model) and add 1 tsp salt and about 20 turns of a black pepper mill. Add the pork joint and turn in the mixture to coat it, then sit it in the pot, skin side down. Cover and cook on low for 7–8 hrs.

2 Meanwhile, make the salad. Mix the carrots with the onion, tomatoes and coriander, then toss just before serving with the lemon juice and oil.

3 Remove the skin and fat from the pork and skim all the fat from the juices, then shred the meat into the juices using two forks. To serve, put some meat and salad on one side of a warmed chapati or wrap, then top with cucumber raita and mango chutney, fold over and eat with your hands.

NUTRITIONAL INFO

PER SERVING KCAL **529** | FAT **24G** | SATURATES **7G** | CARBS **11G** | SUGARS **9G** | FIBRE **7G** | PROTEIN **65G** | SALT **1.1G**

Ham With Sticky Ginger Glaze

Prep: 20 mins
Cook: 7 hrs and 20 mins–7 hrs and 40 mins

Serves 6–8

1 onion, thickly sliced
10 cloves, plus extra for studding
1.3kg (3lb) gammon joint
1.5 litres (2⅔ pints) ginger beer
1 tbsp English mustard, plus extra to serve
3 tbsp ginger preserve
pickled onions, to serve

1 Put the onion and 10 cloves in the base of your slow cooker (we used a 3.5 litre/6 pint model), then nestle in the gammon joint. Pour over the ginger beer, then cover and cook on low for 7 hrs until the gammon is tender, but still holding its shape. You can cool, then keep the gammon chilled in an airtight container for up to 24 hrs at this stage if you like.

2 Heat the oven to 200°C/180°C fan/400°F/Gas Mark 6. Carefully remove the skin from the gammon, leaving a layer of fat behind. Score the fat in a diamond pattern with a sharp knife, making sure you don't cut into the meat, then stud the centre of each diamond with a clove. Sit in a baking dish.

3 Mix the mustard and ginger preserve together in a bowl, spoon or brush over the gammon and bake for 20 mins until golden and sticky. If roasting from cold, you will need to add another 20 mins to the cooking time. Serve hot or cold with mustard and pickled onions.

NUTRITIONAL INFO

PER SERVING (IF SERVING 8) KCAL **363** | FAT **14G** | SATURATES **5G** | CARBS **31G** | SUGARS **30G** | FIBRE **1G** | PROTEIN **27G** | SALT **3.6G**

Smoky Pork with Boston Baked Beans

Prep: 30 mins
Cook: 6 hrs and 40 mins–12 hrs and 40 mins

Serves 8

1–1.5kg (2lb 4oz–3lb 5oz) boneless pork shoulder joint
2 tbsp olive oil
2 onions, finely chopped
1 celery stick, finely chopped
2 garlic cloves, chopped
2 bay leaves
700ml (1¼ pints) passata
700ml (1¼ pints) vegetable stock
2 chipotle chillies or 2–3 tsp chipotle paste
2 tbsp smoked paprika
1 tbsp light brown soft sugar, plus extra to taste
2 tbsp black treacle
2 tbsp balsamic vinegar
3 tbsp Worcestershire sauce, plus extra to taste
750g (1lb 10oz) jar haricot beans, drained

To serve

crusty bread
soured cream
Tabasco sauce (optional)

1 Remove any string from the pork joint and cut away the skin in one piece using a sharp knife. Put the skin on a baking tray, pat dry and season with fine sea salt. Set the pork and skin aside in the fridge.

2 Heat the oil in a large pan over a medium heat. Fry the onions and celery with a pinch of salt for 8 mins until lightly golden. Stir in the garlic and fry for 1 min, then add the remaining ingredients, except the beans. Bring to a simmer and season well, then tip into your slow cooker.

3 Nestle the pork joint into the sauce, cover and cook on high for 6–8 hrs or on low for 10–12 hrs until the pork is very tender and shreds easily. Skim the excess fat from the sauce if you find it sits on top.

4 Shred the pork into the sauce with two forks and stir in the beans. Continue to cook with the lid off for 30 mins or until the sauce is thickened to your liking. Taste and season with salt and pepper, and more Worcestershire sauce and brown sugar, if you like.

5 Meanwhile, heat the oven to 240°C/220°C fan/475°F/Gas Mark 9. Pat the pork skin dry again, score into thin strips with a sharp knife, without cutting all the way through, and cook in the hot oven for 25–30 mins until puffed up and crisp. Break into shards and serve on top of the beans, with crusty bread, soured cream and a dash of Tabasco, if you like.

NUTRITIONAL INFO

PER SERVING KCAL **473** | FAT **22G** | SATURATES **7G** | CARBS **24G** | SUGARS **14G** | FIBRE **9G** | PROTEIN **41G** | SALT **0.71G**

Tender Duck & Pineapple Red Curry

Prep: 20 mins
Cook: 8 hrs and 30 mins

Serves 6

6 skin-on duck legs
2 tbsp light brown soft sugar, plus extra to taste
4 tbsp Thai red curry paste
400ml (14fl oz) coconut milk
2 tbsp fish sauce, plus extra to taste
6 lime leaves
1 small pineapple, peeled, cored and cut into chunks
1 red chilli, deseeded and finely sliced
handful of Thai basil leaves
jasmine rice, to serve

1 Dry-fry the duck legs in a frying pan over a low heat for 10–15 mins, turning once, until coloured all over. Place in your slow cooker with the sugar, curry paste, coconut milk, fish sauce and lime leaves. Cover and cook on high for 8 hrs. Remove the duck, skim any fat off the sauce and stir in the pineapple, half the chilli and half the basil. Cover and cook for 10 mins.

2 Taste and adjust the seasoning if necessary, adding more fish sauce for salt and more sugar for sweetness. Pour the sauce over the duck, then scatter with the rest of the chilli and basil. Serve with jasmine rice.

NUTRITIONAL INFO

PER SERVING KCAL **659** | FAT **49G** | SATURATES **20G** | CARBS **20G** | SUGARS **18G** | FIBRE **2G** | PROTEIN **38G** | SALT **2.29G**

Paella

Prep: 15 mins
Cook: 2 hrs and 20 mins–3 hrs

Serves 4–6

2 tbsp olive oil
4 boneless, skinless chicken thighs, thickly sliced
240g (8½oz) chorizo, thickly sliced
1 onion, sliced
2 garlic cloves, crushed
1 tbsp sweet smoked paprika
pinch of saffron threads (optional)
300g (10½oz) paella rice
150ml (5fl oz) white wine
400g (14oz) can chopped tomatoes
400ml (14fl oz) chicken stock
150g (5½oz) frozen peas
200g (7oz) fresh or frozen peeled raw king prawns, defrosted if frozen
½ small bunch of parsley, finely chopped
lemon wedges, to serve

1 Heat the oil in a frying pan over a medium heat and fry the chicken and chorizo for 7–10 mins until golden. Transfer to your slow cooker. Add the onion to the pan and fry for 5–7 mins or until just softened. Stir in the garlic, paprika and saffron, if using, and cook for 2 mins. Add the rice, pour in the wine and simmer until reduced by half. Tip into the slow cooker with the tomatoes and stock. Season, cover and cook on high for 1 hr 30 mins.

2 Add the peas and prawns and cook for 30 mins more. Check the rice is tender; if not, cook for another 15–30 mins. Scatter over the parsley and serve with lemon wedges for squeezing over.

NUTRITIONAL INFO

PER SERVING (IF SERVING 6) KCAL **517** | FAT **21G** | SATURATES **6G** | CARBS **46G** | SUGARS **7G** | FIBRE **5G** | PROTEIN **31G** | SALT **2G**

V Ve

Pasta e Fagioli

Prep: 20 mins, plus soaking (optional)
Cook: 7–9 hrs

Serves 6–8

200g (7oz) dried borlotti or cannellini beans, or 2 × 400g (14oz) cans, drained and rinsed
2 onions, cut into 1cm (½ inch) chunks
2 carrots, cut into 1cm (½ inch) chunks
3 celery sticks, cut into 1cm (½ inch) chunks
2 tbsp extra virgin olive oil
4 garlic cloves, crushed
1 litre (1¾ pints) vegetable stock
2 tbsp brown rice miso
400g (14oz) can plum tomatoes
6 rosemary sprigs
4 bay leaves
150g (5½oz) ditaloni rigati or other small pasta shapes
200g (7oz) cavolo nero, stalks finely chopped and leaves torn
grated parmesan (or vegetarian alternative), to serve (optional)

1 If using dried beans, soak them for 6–8 hrs in a bowl of cold water. Drain them and bring to the boil in a pan of salted water. Cook for 10 mins, then drain and rinse.

2 Place the beans in your slow cooker with the onions, carrots and celery. Stir in the olive oil, garlic, stock and miso. Add the tomatoes, then half-fill the tomato can with water and add to the pot. Tie the herbs together with kitchen string and add these as well, then season. Cover and cook on low for 6–8 hrs until the beans are cooked through and all of the veg are really tender.

3 Remove and discard the herbs and stir in the pasta. Cover and cook on high for another 30 mins. Add the cavolo nero stalks and leaves and cook for a final 30–40 mins or until the pasta is cooked through and the greens are tender. Serve with grated parmesan, if you like.

NUTRITIONAL INFO

PER SERVING (IF SERVING 8) KCAL **225** | FAT **6G** | SATURATES **1G** | CARBS **29G** | SUGARS **7G** | FIBRE **9G** | PROTEIN **10G** | SALT **0.5G**

V Ve

Healthy Ratatouille

Prep: 10 mins
Cook: 5 hrs and 20 mins–6 hrs and 20 mins

Serves 6

2 tbsp olive oil
1 red onion, sliced
2 garlic cloves, chopped
2 large aubergines, cut into 1.5cm (⅝ inch) pieces
3 courgettes, halved and cut into 2cm (¾ inch) pieces
3 mixed peppers, cut into 2cm (¾ inch) pieces
1 tbsp tomato purée
6 large ripe tomatoes, roughly chopped
small bunch of basil, roughly chopped, plus extra to serve
a few thyme sprigs
400g (14oz) can plum tomatoes
1 tbsp red wine vinegar
1 tsp light brown soft sugar
sourdough, to serve (optional)

1 Heat the oil in a large frying pan and fry the onion for 8 mins until translucent. Add the garlic and fry for 1 min. Turn the heat to medium–high, add the aubergines and fry for 5 mins until golden. Stir in the courgettes and peppers and fry for 5 mins more until slightly soft. Add the remaining ingredients and 1 tsp salt and bring to the boil.

2 Transfer to your slow cooker, cover and cook on low for 5–6 hrs or until everything is soft and the sauce has thickened. Season, scatter over some extra basil and serve with sourdough, if you like.

3 This will keep in the fridge for up to five days.

NUTRITIONAL INFO

PER SERVING KCAL **162** | FAT **5G** | SATURATES **1G** | CARBS **17G** | SUGARS **16G** | FIBRE **11G** | PROTEIN **6G** | SALT **0.8G**

V

Prep: 10 mins
Cook: 3 hrs and 10 mins

Cheesy Creamed Greens

Serves 6–8

50g (1¾oz) butter
½ tbsp olive oil
1 onion, thinly sliced
400g (14oz) cavolo nero, chopped
3 leeks, sliced
100ml (3½fl oz) vegetable stock
400ml (14fl oz) double cream
1 heaped tsp Dijon mustard
generous grating of nutmeg
40g (1½oz) parmesan (or vegetarian alternative), grated

1 Heat the butter and oil in a frying pan. Add the onion and fry for 5 mins over a low heat until softened and translucent. Add the cavolo nero to the pan and fry for 5 mins or until beginning to wilt. Tip into your slow cooker along with the leeks, stock and 300ml (10fl oz) cream. Cover and cook on low for 3 hrs, stirring occasionally.

2 Stir through the remaining cream, the mustard, nutmeg and cheese, as well as some seasoning, just before serving.

3 This will keep, covered, in the fridge for up to three days. Reheat in the slow cooker on medium for 45 mins–1 hr.

NUTRITIONAL INFO

PER SERVING (IF SERVING 8) KCAL **370** | FAT **34G** | SATURATES **21G** | CARBS **7G** | SUGARS **5G** | FIBRE **4G** | PROTEIN **6G** | SALT **0.4G**

Fakeaways

Beef Tacos

Prep: 30 mins
Cook: 6 hrs and 20 mins–8 hrs and 50 mins

Serves 4

1 tbsp vegetable oil
750g–1kg (1lb 10oz–2lb 4oz) brisket, cut into large chunks
about 300ml (10fl oz) beef stock
2 bay leaves

For the spice paste

1 onion, cut into wedges
2 tomatoes, halved
2 garlic cloves, peeled
2 tbsp chipotle paste
1 tsp dried oregano
2 tsp ground cumin
1 tsp ground cinnamon
2 tbsp apple cider vinegar
1 tsp sea salt flakes
½ tsp ground black pepper

To serve

small corn tortillas
guacamole
tomato salsa
hot sauce (optional)
chopped coriander
lime wedges

1 Heat a frying pan over a high heat. For the spice paste, char the onion and tomato pieces for 6–8 mins until blackened slightly and starting to soften, turning every few minutes. This will impart a smoky flavour. Put these and the remaining paste ingredients in a food processor and blitz until smooth.

2 Heat the oil in the same hot pan and fry the brisket for 5–7 mins until golden brown on all sides. Tip in the spice paste and stir for 2–3 mins until fragrant. Transfer to your slow cooker and pour over enough beef stock to cover the meat, then add the bay leaves. Cover and cook on low for 6–8 hrs until the meat is tender. Simmer, uncovered, for an extra 30 mins to reduce the sauce if needed. Check the seasoning.

3 Shred the meat with two forks and stir it back into the thickened sauce. Serve in tortillas, along with guacamole, tomato salsa, hot sauce, if you like, chopped coriander, and lots of lime wedges for squeezing over.

NUTRITIONAL INFO

PER SERVING KCAL **477** | FAT **34G** | SATURATES **13G** | CARBS **5G** | SUGARS **4G** | FIBRE **2G** | PROTEIN **37G** | SALT **1.55G**

Thai Beef Curry

Prep: 20 mins
Cook: 8 hrs and 15 mins

Serves 8

2–3 tbsp groundnut oil

2kg (4lb 8oz) beef short ribs or brisket, cut into large chunks

large bunch of coriander

2 lemongrass stalks, 1 roughly chopped, 1 bashed

3 garlic cloves, chopped

1–2 green chillies, roughly chopped

thumb-sized piece of galangal or ginger, peeled and chopped

50ml (2fl oz) rice wine vinegar

50ml (2fl oz) fish sauce, plus extra to taste

2 tbsp palm or light brown soft sugar, plus extra to taste

400ml (14fl oz) coconut milk

2 star anise

6 lime leaves

juice of 2 limes

To serve

sliced red chilli

coriander

rice

lime wedges

1 Heat a little of the oil in a large pan and brown the beef in batches, removing to a plate and reserving any juices. Meanwhile, in a mini chopper or food processor, whizz half the coriander, the chopped lemongrass, garlic, chillies and galangal or gingerwith the rest of the oil until you have a rough paste.

2 Add the paste to your slow cooker, turn it on to high and heat for a few minutes, then add the beef and all the remaining ingredients, apart from the remaining coriander and the lime juice. Turn the slow cooker to low, cover and cook for 8 hrs or until the meat is very tender.

3 If using beef ribs, remove the bones, then shred the meat with two forks. If the sauce is too thin, strain it off and boil it in a saucepan to reduce. Stir in the remaining coriander and lime juice, then taste and season with more fish sauce or sugar, if you like. At this stage, once cooled, the curry will keep frozen in an airtight container for up to two months. Defrost thoroughly in the fridge and reheat until piping hot.

4 Scatter with red chilli and coriander and serve with rice and lime wedges for squeezing over.

NUTRITIONAL INFO

PER SERVING KCAL **541** | FAT **40G** | SATURATES **20G** | CARBS **10G** | SUGARS **7G** | FIBRE **0G** | PROTEIN **34G** | SALT **1.5G**

Doner Kebab

Prep: 10 mins
Cook: 4 hrs and 10 mins–5 hrs and 10 mins

Serves 4

500g (1lb 2oz) minced lamb (at least 20% fat)
50g (1¾oz) fresh breadcrumbs
1 tsp garlic powder
2 tsp onion powder
2 tsp ground cumin
2 tsp ground coriander
1 tsp smoked paprika
1 tsp dried oregano
½ tsp bicarbonate of soda
3 garlic cloves, crushed
1 tbsp sunflower oil

To serve

flatbreads
garlic sauce
chilli sauce
pickled red onion slices
shredded red cabbage
coriander leaves

1 Tip all the ingredients, except the oil, into a mixing bowl along with 1 tsp fine sea salt and a good few cracks of black pepper. Mix well using your hands, squishing the mixture together until everything is evenly mixed. Tip the mixture out onto a large sheet of foil and bring together into a thick log. Roll up, wrapping the mixture relatively tightly, then fold up the ends. Using a sharp knife, poke several holes in the top of the log.

2 Scrunch up two small bits of foil into little logs and place in your slow cooker. Add the rolled kebab mixture on them with the holes at the top, then pour in a splash of water to just cover the base of the slow cooker. Cover and cook on high for 4–5 hrs.

3 Heat the grill to high. Remove the doner from the slow cooker and transfer to a baking tray. Open out the foil to line the tray and brush the kebab with the oil. Cook under the grill for 6–8 mins until dark brown all over. Hold the doner horizontally and use a serrated knife to slice off thin strips of meat. If you'd like the meat extra crispy, you can brush with a little extra oil and pop under the grill for 2–3 mins. Serve warm with flatbreads, garlic sauce, chilli sauce, pickled red onion slices, shredded red cabbage and coriander.

NUTRITIONAL INFO

PER SERVING KCAL **398** | FAT **29G** | SATURATES **13G** | CARBS **8G** | SUGARS **1G** | FIBRE **3G** | PROTEIN **25G** | SALT **1.91G**

Fall-Apart Barbecue Pork

Prep: 5 mins
Cook: 4–8 hrs

Serves 6–8

1.5kg (3lb 5oz) boneless pork leg or shoulder joint

For the sauce

200ml (7fl oz) barbecue sauce
100ml (3½fl oz) apple cider vinegar
100ml (3½fl oz) chicken stock
1 tbsp dried mixed herbs
1 tsp Dijon mustard
50g (1¾oz) light brown soft sugar
1 tsp garlic granules

To serve

buns
slaw

1. Put all the sauce ingredients in your slow cooker and mix to combine. Add the pork and turn over a few times to coat in the sauce. Cover and cook on high for 4–5 hrs or on low for 7–8 hrs until the pork is easily pulled apart.
2. Remove the pork from the slow cooker and shred it with two forks, then stir the meat back into the sauce. Serve the pork piled into buns topped with slaw.

NUTRITIONAL INFO

PER SERVING (IF SERVING 8) KCAL **382** | FAT **19G** | SATURATES **7G** | CARBS **15G** | SUGARS **12G** | FIBRE **1G** | PROTEIN **37G** | SALT **0.7G**

Tender Pork Ribs

Prep: 10 mins
Cook: 8 hrs and 20 mins–9 hrs and 30 mins

Serves 4

350ml (12fl oz) barbecue sauce
1.5kg (3lb 5oz) meaty pork ribs
2 pork stock cubes
2 bay leaves
1 tsp coriander seeds
1 tsp mustard seeds
1 tsp black peppercorns

1 Put 4 tbsp barbecue sauce in your slow cooker and add the rest of the ingredients. Top up with enough water to cover the meat (about 1.5 litres/2⅔ pints). Cover and cook on low for 8–9 hrs until very tender but not completely falling off the bone.

2 Remove the ribs using tongs and transfer to a foil-lined baking tray. Handle them carefully, as the meat will be very tender and may start to fall off. Baste the ribs with the remaining barbecue sauce.

3 At this point, you can cover the ribs and refrigerate overnight before cooking the following day.

4 Heat the oven to 220°C/200°C fan/425°F/Gas Mark 7. Cook the ribs for 20–30 mins until starting to crisp on the outside. Alternatively, cook on a barbecue, turning from time to time until piping hot.

NUTRITIONAL INFO

PER SERVING KCAL **414** | FAT **24G** | SATURATES **7G** | CARBS **25G** | SUGARS **21G** | FIBRE **1G** | PROTEIN **23G** | SALT **1.9G**

Easy Chicken Curry

Prep: 10 mins, plus marinating
Cook: 6 hrs

Serves 2

1 large onion, roughly chopped
3 tbsp mild curry paste
2 tsp vegetable bouillon powder
1 tbsp finely chopped ginger
1 yellow pepper, chopped
400g (14oz) can chopped tomatoes
2 skinless chicken legs, fat removed
30g (1oz) coriander, leaves chopped
cooked brown rice, to serve

1. Put the onion, curry paste, vegetable bouillon powder, ginger and yellow pepper into your slow cooker. Tip in the chopped tomatoes, then fill the can one-third full with water and add that too. Stir well.
2. Add the chicken legs and push them under the other ingredients so that they are completely submerged. Cover with the lid and chill in the fridge overnight to marinate.
3. The next day, cook on low for 6 hrs until the chicken and vegetables are really tender. Stir in the coriander leaves just before serving the curry over brown rice.

NUTRITIONAL INFO

PER SERVING KCAL **345** | FAT **13G** | SATURATES **2G** | CARBS **24G** | SUGARS **19G** | FIBRE **8G** | PROTEIN **28G** | SALT **2.2G**

Pulled Chicken

Prep: 5 mins
**Cook: 6 hrs and 15 mins–
8 hrs and 15 mins**

Serves 8–10

2 tbsp vegetable or rapeseed oil
10–12 boneless, skinless chicken thighs
2 red onions, sliced
2 garlic cloves, crushed
2 tsp paprika
2 tbsp chipotle paste
250ml (9fl oz) passata
100ml (3½fl oz) barbecue sauce
1 tbsp light brown soft sugar
juice of 1 lime

To serve
burger buns
coriander leaves
sliced chillies
guacamole

1. Heat 1 tbsp oil in a frying pan and brown the chicken in batches, transferring it to your slow cooker as you go. Add the remaining oil to the pan and fry the onions for 5 mins or until just softened, then stir in the garlic and paprika and cook for another minute. Tip into the slow cooker, then swirl 100ml (3½fl oz) water around the pan and pour this in as well.
2. Add the chipotle paste, passata, barbecue sauce, sugar and lime juice, then season and stir. Cover and cook on low for 6–8 hrs until the chicken is really tender. Using two forks, shred the chicken through the sauce. Serve in buns with coriander leaves, sliced chillies and guacamole.

NUTRITIONAL INFO
PER SERVING (IF SERVING 10) KCAL **244** | FAT **11G** | SATURATES **3G** | CARBS **9G** | SUGARS **8G** | FIBRE **1G** | PROTEIN **27G** | SALT **0.35G**

✱

Easy Enchiladas

Prep: 20 mins
Cook: 3 hrs and 15 mins–6 hrs and 15 mins

Serves 4

8 boneless, skinless chicken thighs
1 onion, chopped
3 garlic cloves, chopped
2 red peppers, sliced
200g (7oz) can sweetcorn, drained
2 tbsp smoked paprika
2 tsp chipotle paste
2 tsp ground cumin
250ml (9fl oz) passata
400g (14oz) can black beans, drained and rinsed
8 tortilla wraps
200g (7oz) salsa
200g (7oz) cheddar, grated

To serve

chopped coriander
soured cream
guacamole
salad

1. Put the chicken, onion, garlic, peppers, sweetcorn, paprika, chipotle paste, cumin, passata and beans in your slow cooker and mix well. Cover and cook on high for 3 hrs or on low for 6 hrs.
2. Once cooked, use two forks to shred the chicken and mix into the sauce. Season to taste and leave to cool slightly. At this point, you can refrigerate the chicken mixture overnight and assemble the enchiladas the next day.
3. To assemble the enchiladas, lay the tortillas on a clean chopping board. Using a slotted spoon and, leaving as much liquid behind as possible, spoon the chicken mixture on the tortillas and wrap them up like burritos. Combine the leftover sauce with the salsa, mixing well.
4. If preparing in advance, wrap the enchiladas individually in foil, then tip into a large freezerproof container. Pour the enchilada sauce into a small container and the cheese into another separate small container, then slot the sauce and cheese inside the large container with the enchiladas and keep chilled for 24 hrs or in the freezer for up to three months. If frozen, leave to defrost thoroughly in the fridge before cooking.
5. Heat the oven to 200°C/180°C fan/400°F/Gas Mark 6 and arrange the enchiladas in a large baking dish. Spoon over the enchilada sauce and scatter over the cheese. Cook for 15 mins until golden and bubbling. Serve with chopped coriander, soured cream, guacamole and salad.

NUTRITIONAL INFO

PER SERVING KCAL **794** | FAT **33G** | SATURATES **15G** | CARBS **66G** | SUGARS **11G** | FIBRE **13G** | PROTEIN **51G** | SALT **2.45G**

Chicken Tikka Masala

Prep: 20 mins
Cook: 4 hrs and 30 mins–7 hrs and 30 mins

Serves 4

8–12 boneless,skinless chicken thighs, each cut into 3 chunks
2 tbsp rapeseed oil
1 large onion, chopped
2 garlic cloves, crushed
thumb-sized piece of ginger, peeled and finely grated
3 tbsp tikka curry paste
500ml (18fl oz) passata
1 tbsp tomato purée
1 tbsp malt vinegar, plus extra to taste
1 tbsp light brown soft sugar, plus extra to taste
1 cinnamon stick
5 cardamom pods
100ml (3½fl oz) double cream
handful of chopped coriander, to garnish

To serve
basmati rice
naan
lime wedges

1 Season the chicken, then heat the oil in a wide frying pan over a high heat. Cook the chicken in batches until browned all over, then transfer it to your slow cooker. Add the onion, garlic and ginger to the pan and cook for a few minutes until softened. Add a splash of water and scrape any bits from the bottom of the pan, then tip everything into the slow cooker.

2 Add the remaining ingredients, except the cream and coriander, then season well. Cover and cook on high for 4–5 hrs or on low for 5–7 hrs.

3 Add the cream and check the seasoning, adding more vinegar, sugar or salt if needed. Cook for another 10–15 mins until hot. At this stage, once cooled, the curry will keep frozen in an airtight container for up to two months. Defrost thoroughly in the fridge and reheat until piping hot.

4 Ladle between bowls and garnish with the coriander. Serve with rice, naan and lime wedges for squeezing over.

NUTRITIONAL INFO

PER SERVING KCAL **531** | FAT **33G** | SATURATES **12G** | CARBS **17G** | SUGARS **16G** | FIBRE **4G** | PROTEIN **39G** | SALT **0.75G**

Honey & Garlic Chicken

Prep: 20 mins
Cook: 3 hrs and 10 mins–7 hrs and 10 mins

Serves 4–6

800g (1lb 12oz) boneless, skinless chicken thighs, cut into large chunks
4 garlic cloves, crushed
thumb-sized piece of ginger, peeled and finely grated
3 tbsp honey
3 tbsp soy sauce
3 tbsp tomato ketchup
1 tbsp rice wine or apple cider vinegar
½ tsp chilli flakes (optional)
150ml (5fl oz) chicken stock
1 tbsp cornflour

To serve
egg noodles or rice
roasted peanuts
sliced spring onions

1 Tip the chicken pieces into your slow cooker. Scatter over the garlic and ginger, then stir through the honey, soy sauce, ketchup, vinegar, chilli flakes, if using, and stock to coat the chicken. Cover and cook on high for 3–4 hrs or on low for 6–7 hrs until the chicken is tender but still holding its shape. At this stage, once cooled, the chicken will keep chilled in an airtight container for 24 hrs or frozen for up to three months. Defrost thoroughly in the fridge before reheating until piping hot.

2 Mix the cornflour with 2 tbsp cold water to make a smooth paste, then stir this into the cooking liquid. Cook on high for 10 mins or until the sauce has thickened, stirring occasionally. Serve with egg noodles or rice, scattered with roasted peanuts and sliced spring onions.

NUTRITIONAL INFO

PER SERVING (IF SERVING 6) KCAL **246** | FAT **9G** | SATURATES **2G** | CARBS **15G** | SUGARS **12G** | FIBRE **0.3G** | PROTEIN **27G** | SALT **1.81G**

Chicken Korma

Prep: 15 mins
Cook: 5 hrs and 20 mins–6 hrs and 30 mins

Serves 4–6

2 garlic cloves, peeled
thumb-sized piece of ginger, peeled
2 large onions, finely chopped
2 tbsp vegetable oil
6 boneless, skinless chicken breasts, cut into large chunks
2 tbsp tomato purée
1 tsp ground cumin
1 tsp paprika
1 tsp ground turmeric
1 tsp ground coriander
¼–½ tsp chilli powder
2 tsp golden caster sugar
300ml (10fl oz) chicken stock
150ml (5fl oz) double cream
6 tbsp ground almonds

To serve

toasted flaked almonds
chopped coriander
cooked basmati rice
naan

1 Put the garlic, ginger and onions in a small blender with a splash of water and whizz to a paste. Heat the oil in a frying pan over a medium–high heat and sear the chicken all over. Remove from the pan and set aside, then add the onion paste. Fry the paste over a medium heat for 10 mins until lightly golden.

2 Stir in the tomato purée, spices, 1 tsp salt and the sugar and fry for 1 min until aromatic, then put the chicken back into the pan (with any resting juices) and add the stock. Stir and bring to a simmer, then transfer to your slow cooker. Cover and cook on low for 5–6 hrs until the chicken is tender and cooked through.

3 Stir through the cream and the ground almonds and bubble for 10 mins to reduce, if needed. At this stage, once cooled, the korma will keep frozen in an airtight container for up to two months. Defrost thoroughly in the fridge and reheat until piping hot.

4 Scatter with toasted flaked almonds and coriander and serve with cooked basmati rice and naan.

NUTRITIONAL INFO

PER SERVING (IF SERVING 6) KCAL **499** | FAT **33G** | SATURATES **11G** | CARBS **7G** | SUGARS **6G** | FIBRE **2G** | PROTEIN **43G** | SALT **1.4G**

Turkey Pho

Prep: 20 mins
Cook: 8 hrs and 10 mins–10 hrs and 10 mins

Serves 4

200g (7oz) flat rice noodles
400g (14oz) cooked turkey or chicken, sliced
100g (3½oz) beansprouts or shredded carrot, mooli or Brussels sprouts
handful of Thai basil, mint and coriander leaves
2 red chillies, finely sliced

For the stock

50g (1¾oz) ginger, peeled and thickly sliced
2 onions, halved
3 star anise
2 cinnamon sticks
½ tbsp coriander seeds
2 cloves
1 turkey or chicken carcass, meat removed
2–3 tbsp fish sauce
2 tbsp golden caster sugar

To serve

1 lime, cut into wedges
hoisin sauce
sriracha sauce

1 To make the stock, fry the ginger and onions in a dry frying pan over a high heat until deeply coloured. Transfer to your slow cooker. Fry the whole spices for a few minutes until fragrant, then tip into the slow cooker. If pressed for time, simply put in the slow cooker without frying.

2 Add the carcass, then pour 3–4 litres (5¼–7 pints) boiling water into the cooker so that the bones are covered, ensuring you don't overfill it. Cover and cook on low for 8–10 hrs, depending on how much time you have.

3 Strain the stock, discarding the bones and spices. Season with the fish sauce and sugar. At this point, you can leave the stock to cool completely and freeze in an airtight container for up to three months. Defrost thoroughly in the fridge and reheat until piping hot.

4 Cook the noodles following pack instructions, drain and divide between bowls. Top with the turkey and beansprouts or veg, then cover with the hot stock. Scatter over the herbs and chillies, then serve with the lime wedges for squeezing over and the sauces.

NUTRITIONAL INFO

PER SERVING KCAL **334** | FAT **6G** | SATURATES **2G** | CARBS **36G** | SUGARS **8G** | FIBRE **4G** | PROTEIN **33G** | SALT **1.9G**

✱ V

Prep: 35 mins, plus soaking
Cook: 5 hrs and 15 mins–6 hrs and 15 mins

Creamy Dhal with Crispy Onions

Serves 4

250g (9oz) dried black urid beans or yellow split peas
100g (3½oz) butter or ghee
2 large onions, thinly sliced
3 garlic cloves, crushed
thumb-sized piece of ginger, peeled and finely chopped
2 tsp ground cumin
2 tsp ground coriander
1 tsp ground turmeric
1 tsp paprika
¼ tsp chilli powder (optional)
small bunch of coriander, finely chopped
400ml (14fl oz) passata or canned chopped tomatoes
1 fat red chilli, pierced a few times with a sharp knife
50ml (2fl oz) double cream
naan, to serve

For the crispy onions (optional)
vegetable or sunflower oil
1 onion, thinly sliced

1. Soak the beans or split peas in cold water for 4 hrs or overnight.
2. Melt the butter or ghee in a large pan over a low heat, then add the onions, garlic and ginger and cook for 10–15 mins until the onions are starting to caramelize. Stir in the spices, chopped coriander and 100ml (3½fl oz) water. Pour into your slow cooker and add the passata or chopped tomatoes and whole red chilli. Drain the beans or split peas and add these too, then top up with 400ml (14fl oz) water. Season well, cover and cook on low for 5–6 hrs.
3. If you are making the crispy onions, heat enough vegetable or sunflower oil to come 1–2 cm (½–¾ inch) up the sides of a large pan. When hot, fry the onion in batches until crisp, drain on kitchen paper and sprinkle with salt.
4. Once cooked, the dhal should be very thick and the beans or split peas should be tender. Stir in the cream, check the seasoning and serve in bowls with the crispy onions, if you like, and naan.
5. Once cooled, the dhal will keep chilled in an airtight container for 24 hrs or frozen for up to two months. Defrost thoroughly in the fridge before reheating until piping hot.

NUTRITIONAL INFO

PER SERVING KCAL **527** | FAT **34G** | SATURATES **21G** | CARBS **35G** | SUGARS **9G** | FIBRE **6G** | PROTEIN **19G** | SALT **0.1G**

Desserts & Bakes

V

Sticky Toffee Pudding

Prep: 10 mins, plus soaking
Cook: 7–8 hrs

Serves 8

250g (9oz) pitted dates, chopped
100g (3½oz) butter, plus extra for greasing
4 tbsp treacle
1 tsp vanilla extract
250g (9oz) light brown soft sugar
300ml (10fl oz) double cream
2 eggs, beaten
200g (7oz) self-raising flour
1 tsp bicarbonate of soda
ice cream, to serve

1 Put the dates in a heatproof bowl, cover with 150ml (5fl oz) boiling water and leave to soak for 30 mins. Butter a 1 litre (1¾ pint) pudding basin and line the base with baking parchment.

2 Tip half the butter, half the treacle, the vanilla, 75g (2¾oz) sugar and the cream into a pan set over a medium heat. Cook for 4–5 mins, stirring, until the sugar dissolves. Turn up the heat and bubble for 3 mins, then whisk in a pinch of salt. Pour one-third of the sauce into the basin.

3 Beat the remaining butter, treacle and sugar together with the eggs, then fold in the flour, bicarb, ¼ tsp salt and the dates and their soaking liquid. Spoon into the basin and smooth the surface, leaving a 1cm (½ inch) gap at the top. Cover with a double layer of baking parchment and foil, making a pleat in the middle so that the pudding can expand. Secure with kitchen string.

4 Sit the basin inside your slow cooker, then add enough boiling water to come halfway up the sides of the basin. Cover and cook on low for 7–8 hrs. Run a knife around the edge of the pudding and turn out onto a plate. Reheat the remaining sauce and pour over. Serve with ice cream.

NUTRITIONAL INFO

PER SERVING KCAL **625** | FAT **32G** | SATURATES **19G** | CARBS **76G** | SUGARS **58G** | FIBRE **3G** | PROTEIN **6G** | SALT **1.03G**

V Ve

Prep: 20 mins
Cook: 8–10 hrs

Apple, Pear & Cherry Compote

Serves 12

8 eating apples, peeled, cored and cut into chunks
4 Bramley apples, peeled, cored and cut into chunks
8 firm pears, peeled, cored and thickly sliced
6 tbsp golden caster sugar, plus extra to taste
280g (10oz) dried sour cherries or cranberries
vanilla ice cream, to serve (optional)

1 Put the apples, pears, sugar and cherries into your slow cooker with 50ml (2fl oz) water and give it a good stir. Cover and cook on low for 8–10 hrs until the Bramley apples have collapsed to a purée and the pears and eating apples are tender.

2 Taste and add a little more sugar if necessary. Once cooled, this can be kept chilled in an airtight container for up to five days. Serve with vanilla ice cream, if you like.

NUTRITIONAL INFO

PER SERVING KCAL **199** | FAT **1G** | SATURATES **0G** | CARBS **51G** | SUGARS **47G** | FIBRE **4G** | PROTEIN **1G** | SALT **0.03G**

V

Prep: 15 mins
Cook: 2 hrs and 35 mins

Old-School Rice Pudding

Serves 6

1 tsp butter
1 litre (1¾ pints) milk
200g (7oz) wholegrain pudding rice
pinch of grated nutmeg or ground cinnamon

To serve

honey
toasted flaked almonds

1. Butter your slow cooker all over the base and halfway up the sides. Heat the milk to simmering point in a saucepan. Mix the pudding rice with the milk and pour it into the slow cooker. Add the nutmeg or cinnamon, cover and cook on high for 2 hrs 30 mins, stirring once or twice if you can.
2. Serve with honey and toasted flaked almonds.

NUTRITIONAL INFO

PER SERVING KCAL **200** | FAT **4G** | SATURATES **2G** | CARBS **32G** | SUGARS **8G** | FIBRE **1G** | PROTEIN **8G** | SALT **0.2G**

V

Prep: 30 mins, plus cooling and chilling
Cook: 2 hrs and 10 mins

Muscovado Cheesecake with Hazelnuts & Blackberries

Serves 10

- 50g (1¾oz) butter, melted, plus extra for greasing
- 225g (8oz) oat biscuits
- 100g (3½oz) blanched hazelnuts
- 250g (9oz) light muscovado sugar
- 4 tbsp whole milk
- 750g (1lb 10oz) full-fat soft cheese
- 2 tbsp plain flour
- 1 tsp vanilla extract
- 3 large eggs
- 200ml (7fl oz) soured cream
- 1 tbsp Frangelico or other hazelnut liqueur, plus extra to serve (optional)
- 2 tsp cornflour
- 3 tbsp golden caster sugar
- 200g (7oz) blackberries

1 Boil the kettle and prepare your slow cooker (it needs to be at least 22cm/8½ inches wide). Make a trivet for your cheesecake by scrunching a long piece of foil into a sausage. Roll into a loose coil and put in the bottom of the slow cooker. Turn the slow cooker to high and pour in enough hot water to come 4cm (1½ inches) up the sides. Wrap the outside of a 20cm (8 inch) springform cake tin in a large sheet of baking parchment and then foil – make sure there are no gaps for water to seep in. Grease the inside with butter and line with another large sheet of baking parchment (scrunching the parchment up first, then flattening it back out will help it fit into the corners).

2 Tip the biscuits and 50g (1¾oz) hazelnuts into a food processer and blitz to fine crumbs. Add the melted butter and blend again until well combined. Tip the crumbs into the tin and use a spoon to press into an even layer in the base. Chill for 10 mins.

3 In a saucepan, heat the muscovado and milk until the sugar has dissolved. Set aside to cool. In a bowl, beat the soft cheese, flour, vanilla and eggs until smooth. Stir in the soured cream, liqueur, if using, and cooled sugar mixture until well combined. Pour into the tin and carefully put it in the slow cooker. Wrap the lid in a tea towel to prevent condensation from dripping onto the cheesecake. Cover and cook for 2 hrs, then turn off the slow cooker. Leave the cheesecake inside without opening for another 2 hrs. Remove from the slow cooker and cool at room temperature for a further 1 hr, then chill for 4 hrs or overnight.

4 Put the cornflour, caster sugar and half the blackberries in a saucepan and set over a high heat. Cook for 3–4 mins, squashing the blackberries a little, until syrupy. Toss in the remaining berries and heat through, then remove from the heat and cool until you're ready to serve. Roughly chop the remaining nuts and toast in a frying pan.

5 To serve, carefully remove the cheesecake from the tin, remove the baking parchment and transfer to a plate or cake stand. Top with the berries and hazelnuts and serve with a shot of the liqueur, if you like.

NUTRITIONAL INFO

PER SERVING KCAL **612** | FAT **39G** | SATURATES **19G** | CARBS **52G** | SUGARS **40G** | FIBRE **3G** | PROTEIN **10G** | SALT **0.8G**

V

Prep: 15 mins
Cook: 2 hrs

Spiced Apples with Barley

Serves 4

100g (3½ oz) pearl barley
2 eating apples
½ tsp ground cinnamon
pinch of grated nutmeg
finely grated zest of 1 large orange
4 tbsp natural yogurt

1 Put the barley and 750ml (1⅓ pints) boiling water into your slow cooker. Peel and core the apples so that you have a hole through the middle of each one. Cut each apple in half.

2 Arrange the apples, cut sides up, on the barley. Mix the cinnamon, nutmeg and orange zest together, then sprinkle over the apples. Cover and cook on low for 2 hrs, then serve with the yogurt.

NUTRITIONAL INFO

PER SERVING KCAL **168** | FAT **2G** | SATURATES **1G** | CARBS **28G** | SUGARS **15G** | FIBRE **6G** | PROTEIN **6G** | SALT **0.1G**

V

Prep: 20 mins
Cook: 2 hrs and 30 mins–4 hrs and 35 mins

Apple Flapjack Crumble

Serves 6

1.1kg (2lb 7oz) eating apples, such as Cox, peeled and thinly sliced
3–4 tbsp apricot jam
juice of 1 large orange
custard, cream or ice cream, to serve

For the crumble

140g (5oz) porridge oats
100g (3½oz) plain flour
1 tsp ground cinnamon
100g (3½oz) butter, cut into small cubes
100g (3½oz) light muscovado sugar
1 tbsp golden syrup

1 Mix the sliced apples with the jam and orange juice in your slow cooker. Cover and cook on low for 2–4 hrs until tender.

2 Mix the oats, flour and cinnamon in a large bowl. Add the butter and rub in gently. Stir in the sugar and rub in again. Drizzle over the syrup, mixing with a round-bladed knife so that it forms small clumps.

3 Heat the oven to 190°C/fan 170°C/375°F/Gas Mark 5. Transfer the apple mixture to a baking dish and top with the crumble. Bake for 30–35 mins until the juices from the apples start to bubble up. Cool for 10 mins, then serve with custard, cream or ice cream.

NUTRITIONAL INFO

PER SERVING KCAL **447** | FAT **16G** | SATURATES **9G** | CARBS **75G** | SUGARS **45G** | FIBRE **6G** | PROTEIN **6G** | SALT **0.33G**

V

Prep: 30 mins, plus soaking
Cook: 14 hrs

Rich & Sticky Christmas Pudding

Serves 10

100g (3½oz) sultanas
100g (3½oz) raisins
100g (3½oz) currants
30g (1oz) mixed candied peel, chopped
1 small cooking apple, peeled, cored and finely chopped
zest of 2 oranges and juice of 1
zest of 2 lemons
5 tablespoons brandy, whisky or rum
100ml (3½fl oz) stout
2 eggs
100g (3½oz) shredded suet
50g (1¾oz) self-raising flour
100g (3½oz) fresh breadcrumbs
1 tsp ground mixed spice
1 tsp ground cinnamon
200g (7oz) dark brown soft sugar
50g (1¾oz) whole blanched almonds, chopped
butter, for greasing

To serve

triple sec (optional)
brandy butter
custard

1. Tip the sultanas, raisins, currants and candied peel into the largest bowl you have. Add the apple, citrus zests, orange juice, spirit and stout. Stir everything together, cover with a clean tea towel and leave overnight to soak.
2. Add all the remaining ingredients to the bowl along with ½ tsp salt and mix well to combine – don't forget to make a wish!
3. Butter a 1 litre (1¾ pint) pudding basin and line the base with a circle of baking parchment. Spoon in the pudding mixture, pressing it down well, then make a hollow in the middle using the back of the spoon. Cover the surface with another circle of baking parchment, then lay a sheet of parchment on a sheet of foil, fold a pleat in the middle and use this to cover the basin. Secure at the rim with kitchen string and add a looped handle. Carefully lower the basin into your slow cooker, then fill with water so that it comes halfway up the sides of the basin. Cover and cook on low for 10 hrs, topping up with water as necessary. Once cooked, remove the basin from the slow cooker and leave to cool completely before storing in a cool, dark place for up to six months.
4. On the day you're ready to serve, return the pudding to the slow cooker and fill with water as before. Reheat on low for 4 hrs, then turn out onto a serving plate. If you like, warm some triple sec in a small pan over a low heat, drizzle this over the pudding and carefully set alight. Serve with brandy butter and custard.

NUTRITIONAL INFO

PER SERVING KCAL **371** | FAT **13G** | SATURATES **6G** | CARBS **52G** | SUGARS **42G** | FIBRE **2G** | PROTEIN **5G** | SALT **0.51G**

V

Self-Saucing Pud

Prep: 20 mins
Cook: 1 hr and 30 mins–2 hrs and 30 mins

Serves 6–8

100g (3½oz) butter, melted, plus extra for greasing
125g (4½oz) golden caster sugar
100g (3½oz) light brown soft sugar
2 eggs
200ml (7fl oz) milk
275g (9¾oz) self-raising flour
½ tsp baking powder
1½ tbsp ground ginger
1 tsp ground cinnamon
double cream, to serve (optional)

For the sauce
1 tbsp cornflour
175g (6oz) light brown soft sugar
1 tbsp ground ginger

1. Heat the slow cooker on high for 20 mins. Carefully rub the basin of your slow cooker with butter.
2. Make the sponge by combining the melted butter with both sugars, the eggs and milk, then fold in the flour, baking powder, ginger and cinnamon. Whisk to remove any lumps if needed, then pour into your slow cooker.
3. For the sauce, mix the cornflour with 1 tsp water, then set aside. Combine the sugar and ginger with 350ml (12fl oz) boiling water until the sugar has dissolved. Mix in the cornflour paste, then pour over the batter.
4. Cover and cook on high for 1 hr 30 mins–2 hours 30 mins (this will vary depending on your slow cooker) until the sponge has set and is firm to the touch. To serve, pour over some double cream, if you like.

NUTRITIONAL INFO
PER SERVING (IF SERVING 8) KCAL **463** | FAT **13G** | SATURATES **8G** | CARBS **79G** | SUGARS **51G** | FIBRE **2G** | PROTEIN **6G** | SALT **0.71G**

V

Prep: 25 mins
Cook: 3–6 hrs

Hot Chocolate Fondant Cake

Serves 8

100g (3½oz) butter, plus extra for greasing
100g (3½oz) golden caster sugar
50g (1¾oz) light brown soft sugar
3 eggs
250g (9oz) self-raising flour
50g (1¾oz) cocoa powder
1 tsp baking powder
½ tsp instant espresso powder
100g (3½oz) dark chocolate (70% cocoa solids), chopped
100–150ml (3½–5fl oz) milk
crème fraîche, whipped cream or vanilla ice cream, to serve

For the sauce

200g (7oz) light brown soft sugar
25g (1oz) cocoa powder
½ tsp instant espresso powder
½ tsp vanilla extract

1 Butter the base and sides of the bowl of your slow cooker. Beat the butter and both sugars together in a stand mixer with the whisk attachment or using an electric whisk until pale and fluffy. Add the eggs, one at a time, then fold in the flour, cocoa powder, baking powder, espresso, a pinch of salt and the chocolate. Add just enough milk so that the batter falls off the spatula in big dollops. Spoon into the slow cooker.

2 Mix the sauce ingredients together in a heatproof bowl with 300ml (10fl oz) boiling water, then carefully pour this over the batter in the slow cooker. Cover and cook on high for 3 hrs or on low for 5–6 hrs until the cake springs back when pressed and is well risen. Serve with crème fraîche, whipped cream or vanilla ice cream.

NUTRITIONAL INFO

PER SERVING KCAL **518** | FAT **20G** | SATURATES **11G** | CARBS **74G** | SUGARS **48G** | FIBRE **4G** | PROTEIN **9G** | SALT **0.8G**

✳ V

Banana Bread

Prep: 15 mins
Cook: 3 hrs and 30 mins–3 hrs and 45 mins

Serves 8–10

150g (5½oz) butter, softened, plus extra to serve (optional)
100g (3½oz) golden caster sugar
100g (3½oz) light brown soft sugar
3 eggs
250g (9oz) self-raising flour
1 tsp baking powder
3 ripe bananas (about 300g/10½oz peeled weight), mashed

1 Line the base and the bottom 5cm (2 inches) of the sides of your slow cooker with foil to create a kind of cake tin, then line the foil with baking parchment.

2 Beat the butter and both sugars together in a stand mixer with the whisk attachment or using an electric whisk until light and creamy – this should take about 5 mins. Beat in 1 egg with a spoonful of the flour until combined. Repeat until all the eggs have been incorporated.

3 Fold in the remaining flour and baking powder followed by the mashed bananas, then tip into the slow cooker. Cover and cook on high for 3 hrs 30 mins, then check to see if it's done. A skewer inserted into the middle should come out clean. If not, put the lid back on and cook for another 15 mins, then check again.

4 Turn out onto a bread board and leave to cool before serving with a little butter, or just as it is.

5 You can freeze any leftovers in an airtight container for up to two months. Defrost thoroughly at room temperature before serving.

NUTRITIONAL INFO

PER SERVING (IF SERVING 10) KCAL **328** | FAT **14G** | SATURATES **8G** | CARBS **45G** | SUGARS **25G** | FIBRE **1G** | PROTEIN **5G** | SALT **0.7G**

V

Prep: 5 mins
Cook: 2 hrs and 20 mins

Hot Chocolate

Serves 8–10

1 litre (1¾ pints) milk
300ml (10fl oz) double cream
200g (7oz) dark chocolate (70% cocoa solids), chopped, plus extra, grated, to serve
100g (3½oz) milk chocolate, chopped

To serve

scorched marshmallows
softly whipped cream

TIP

You can add 25ml (1½ tbsp) of your favourite liqueur or spirit to each mug for a warming kick.

1 Pour the milk and double cream into your slow cooker. Add the dark chocolate and milk chocolate, then cover and cook on low for 2 hrs, stirring halfway through cooking.

2 Remove the lid and stir again, then cover and continue to cook for a further 15–20 mins. Ladle into mugs and top with scorched marshmallows, whipped cream and grated dark chocolate.

NUTRITIONAL INFO

PER SERVING (IF SERVING 10) KCAL **337** | FAT **30G** | SATURATES **19G** | CARBS **19G** | SUGARS **17G** | FIBRE **2G** | PROTEIN **6G** | SALT **0.15G**

V

Easy Chocolate Fudge

Prep: 10 mins, plus chilling
Cook: 1 hr

Makes 36 squares

375g (13oz) can condensed milk
250g (9oz) milk chocolate, chopped
250g (9oz) dark chocolate (70% cocoa solids), chopped
100g (3½oz) light brown soft sugar
1 tsp vanilla extract
vegetable oil, for greasing

1 Set your slow cooker to low (we used a 6 litre/10½ pint model). Tip in the condensed milk, both chocolates, the sugar, vanilla and a pinch of salt. Cover and cook for 1 hr, stirring well with a spatula every 15 mins to combine and scrape off any bits that start to stick to the bowl, until thick and smooth.

2 Oil a 20cm (8 inch) square tin, then line with baking parchment. Pour the fudge mixture into the tin and chill for 4 hrs.

3 Cut the fudge into 36 squares using a sharp knife. This will keep in an airtight container in the fridge for three days.

NUTRITIONAL INFO

PER SQUARE KCAL **120** | FAT **6G** | SATURATES **3G** | CARBS **14G** | SUGARS **14G** | FIBRE **1G** | PROTEIN **2G** | SALT **0.06G**

Index

Index

UK/US Glossary

aubergine – eggplant

bacon lardons – matchsticks of slab bacon

bacon rasher – slice of bacon

baking parchment – wax paper/parchment paper

baking tray – baking sheet

bicarbonate of soda – baking soda

broad beans – fava beans

butter beans – lima beans

cavolo nero – Tuscan kale

celeriac – celery root

chickpeas – garbanzo beans

chilli flakes – red pepper flakes

chopping board – cutting board

coriander (fresh) – cilantro

cornflour – cornstarch

courgette – zucchini

crème fraîche – if unavailable, use sour cream

dark chocolate – semi-sweet chocolate

dark muscovado sugar – if unavailable, use regular dark brown sugar

double cream – heavy cream

flaked almonds – sliced almonds

foil – aluminium foil

frying pan – skillet

gammon joint – raw ham joint

golden caster sugar – if unavailable, use white superfine sugar

grated – shredded

grill – broil/broiler

groundnut oil – peanut oil

haricot beans – navy beans

hob – stove

jug – pitcher

king prawn – jumbo shrimp

kitchen paper – paper towels

light muscovado sugar – if unavailable, use regular light brown sugar

minced meat – ground meat

mooli – daikon

natural yogurt – plain yogurt

passata – strained tomatoes

peppers (green/red/yellow) – bell peppers

plain flour – all-purpose flour

prawn – shrimp

rapeseed oil – canola oil

roasting tin – roasting pan

self-raising flour – self-rising flour

semi-skimmed milk – reduced-fat milk

sieve – fine-mesh strainer

single cream – light cream

soured cream – sour cream

spring onions – green onions/scallions

stock – broth

streaky bacon – bacon

sultanas – golden raisins

sweetcorn – corn

tea towel – dish towel

tomato purée – tomato paste